Collins
English for Life

A2 Pre-intermediate

Speaking

Rhona Snelling

Collins

HarperCollins Publishers
1 London Bridge Street
London
SE1 9EF

HarperCollins Publishers
1st Floor, Watermarque Building
Ringsend Road
Dublin 4, Ireland

First edition 2013

10 9 8

© HarperCollins Publishers 2013

ISBN 978-0-00-749777-5

Collins® is a registered trademark of HarperCollins
Publishers Limited.

www.collins.co.uk/elt
www.collinsdictionary.com

A catalogue record for this book is available from

the British Library.

Typeset in India by Aptara

Printed and bound in the UK using 100% Renewable
Electricity at CPI Group (UK) Ltd

About the author

Rhona Snelling is a freelance ELT writer and editor, with extensive experience of teaching exam courses in private language schools and universities in the UK and overseas. She has a Master's degree in Applied Linguistics from the University of Oxford and is the author of *Get Ready for IELTS: Speaking* (Collins, 2012).

CONTENTS

INTRODUCTION

Collins English for Life: Speaking will help you to improve your spoken English in a variety of everyday situations and contexts.

You can use *Speaking*:
- as a self-study course
- as supplementary material on a general English course.

Speaking will help you develop your speaking skills in different areas, including:
- introductions with new people and describing people, things and places
- making and responding to arrangements
- ordering and buying
- speaking on the phone
- developing conversations and checking for understanding
- making a request, a complaint and an apology
- listening to problems and showing sympathy
- saying 'thank you' and 'well done!'
- agreeing and disagreeing, and giving feedback.

Speaking comprises a **book** and **audio**. The book has 20 units.
At the back of the book there is:
- a mini-dictionary taken from Collins COBUILD dictionaries
- an answer key
- the script for the audio recordings.

There are over 100 tracks of audio including conversations and speaking practice activities.

Using *Speaking*

You can either work through the units from Unit 1 to Unit 20, or you can choose the units that are most useful to you. The Contents page will help you in your selection of units and your own plan for learning.

For ease of use, each of the 20 units follows the same format. It is recommended that you follow the order of exercises when working through a unit. Each unit includes all or most of the following:

Conversations – you read and listen to conversations. Key words and phrases are presented in bold. You check your understanding of the conversation and the key words and phrases.

Say it accurately – you practise using the key words and phrases correctly.

Say it clearly – you practise pronouncing the correct sounds and words. For example, linking words together.

Say it appropriately – you practise using tone and suitable intonation. For example, sounding polite.

Get speaking – you practise using the key words and phrases in spoken exercises. Instructions are provided to prepare you for role-plays with speakers from the audio.

There are also:

Useful tips – these explain how to use language in particular situations.

Language notes – these help you be clear on grammar and language areas. Language notes may explain the meaning of a phrase or the differences between words and phrases that sound similar.

Study tips

- Each unit should take about 30–45 minutes to work through. Take regular breaks and do not try to study for long periods of time. Thirty minutes is a good length for one study session.
- At the start of every study session, quickly revise your last study session. Check you remember and understand the language.
- Put the audio tracks on your mobile phone, so you can listen to the conversations and practice activities at any time.
- Use the book and audio with a classmate. Work through each exercise together, or work through each exercise individually and then compare your answers.
- Complete the **Get speaking** section as pair work: one student reads the Audio script and one student responds following the instructions in the book.
- Test yourself with previous units – close your book. Play the audio from the **Get speaking** section and give your response. Check your responses with the unit and the model answers at the back of the book.
- Use your mobile phone to record yourself giving answers out loud. Listen carefully to your answers – compare your pronunciation, tone and intonation with the **audio tracks**.
- Keep good study records – choose the best method for you to record and revise new vocabulary and grammar. For example, using mind maps for new topic vocabulary.

Language level

Speaking has been written to help learners at A2 level and above (Elementary to Pre-Intermediate).

Other titles

Also available in the *Collins English for Life* series at A2 level: *Listening*, *Reading*, and *Writing*.

Available in the *Collins English for Life* series at B1+ level: *Speaking*, *Listening*, *Reading*, and *Writing*.

Using the audio
This icon indicates there is an audio track for the exercise. You can download the audio files at **www.collins.co.uk/eltresources**.

---

1 MEETING PEOPLE

Getting started

1 Where are the people in the photo?
2 Are they meeting for the first time or are they friends?
3 What do you usually say when you meet someone?

Conversations

01

1 Read and listen to these four conversations. Which conversations include people who know each other? Which include people meeting for the first time?

Know each other: ....

Meeting for the first time: ....

Conversation 1

Clare:	Hi Sarah, **it's great to see you.**
Sarah:	Hiya, **and you.** It's been ages. You look well.
Clare:	Thanks, you too. **How are you doing?**
Sarah:	**Very well.** I've got a new job. I'm teaching at the college.
Clare:	Great! You didn't like your old job, did you?
Sarah:	No, I hated it. **What's your news?**
Clare:	Well, I'm getting married next year.
Sarah:	Congratulations!

Conversation 2

Receptionist:	Good afternoon. How can I help you?
Sam:	Good afternoon, my name's Sam Jones. I have a meeting with Mr Williams at 3 p.m.
Receptionist:	Ah, yes. Please take a seat. I'll let Mr Williams know you're here. ...
Mr Williams:	Ms Jones? I'm Tom Williams. **Lovely to meet you.**
Sam:	**And you,** Mr Williams.
Mr Williams:	**How was your journey?** Was the traffic OK?
Sam:	Yes, everything was fine, thanks.

Conversation 3

Andy: Hey, **how are things?**

Ben: **Good, thanks.** You? Have you finished that essay?

Andy: No, not yet. It's really difficult, isn't it? **Sorry, do you know** Karen? She's in my sister's class. Karen, Ben. Ben, Karen.

Ben: Hi, **nice to meet you.**

Karen: You too.

Conversation 4

Tony: Good morning, Mark. **Good to see you again.**

Mark: Morning, Tony. You too.

Tony: Mark, **let me introduce you to** Tina. She's doing an internship here for the summer. Tina, this is Mark. He runs our new office in Bristol.

Mark: **Pleased to meet you**, Tina.

Tina: And you, Tony.

Mark: **How are you finding it here?** It's very busy, isn't it?

Tina: Yes, it is. But I'm really enjoying it, thanks.

Useful tip: introducing friends

Notice how friends introduce each other: 'Karen, Ben. Ben, Karen'. You don't have to use phrases:

Karen, this is Ben. Ben, this is Karen.

② Read and listen to the four conversations again. Complete the sentences below with the correct name.

1 .... is getting married.

2 .... has a new job.

3 .... has a meeting with Sam Jones.

4 .... had a good journey.

5 .... hasn't finished an essay.

6 .... is in Andy's sister's class.

7 .... is doing an internship.

8 .... works in the new office.

Language note

Question tags are very common in spoken English. Remember to use a negative question tag after a positive sentence:

*It's very busy, **isn't it?***

Remember to use a positive question tag after a negative sentence:

*You **didn't** like your old job, **did you?***

3 Look at the bold words in the conversations. Complete the phrases below.

Meeting someone you don't know	1	L..................................... to meet you.		
	2	P..................................... to meet you.		
	3	N..................................... to meet you.	4	You t....................
Introducing someone	5	Let me i..................................... you to ...		
	6	Sorry, do you k..................................... ...		
Asking a follow up question	7	What's your n.....................................?		
	8	How was your j.....................................?		
	9	How are you f..................................... it here?		

Saying it accurately

1 Read the conversation below and complete the gaps with words from Conversations, exercise 3.

Ana: Good afternoon, Katy. Good to see you again.

Katy: And you, Ana.

Ana: Katy, 1 .... me introduce you to Lucy. She's working with me on a new project. Lucy, 2 .... is Amy. She joined the company about a month ago.

Katy: 3 .... to meet you, Lucy.

Lucy: You 4 ....

2 Put the sentences in the correct order to make a conversation.

Paul: I'm very well, thanks. How was your journey? ....

Gary: Good, thanks. How are you doing? ....

Paul: Hiya, you too. How are things? ....

Gary: OK, thanks. The train was on time. ....

Gary: Hi, Paul. It's great to see you.   *1*

3 Listen and check.

Saying it clearly

1 In spoken English, some words 'link' together. This means the sound at the end of one word links with the sound at the beginning of the next word. Listen to the phrases below and pay attention to the words that 'link' together.

1 How_are things?

2 Sorry, do_you know ... ?

3 How_was your journey?

4 What's_your news?

2 Listen again and repeat the phrases. Try to join the words together.

3   Write an answer for each question in exercise 1. Then practise saying the question and answer to improve your pronunciation.

1 ....   3 ....

2 ....   4 ....

Saying it appropriately

04   **1**   You're going to hear two people saying the sentences below. Which speaker sounds interested? Put a tick (✓) in the correct column.

		1	**2**
1	How are you doing?	✓	....
2	What's your news?	....	....
3	It's great to see you.	....	....
4	Lovely to meet you.	....	....
5	And you.	....	....
6	Nice to meet you.	....	....
7	You too.	....	....
8	How was your journey?	....	....

05   **2**   Listen to the speakers who sound interested. Repeat each sentence. Listen again and repeat to improve your intonation.

Useful tip: meeting someone new

Remember to sound interested when meeting someone new. It is as important as eye contact and shaking hands or giving a kiss.

Get speaking

06   **1**   Listen to speakers 1–4 and choose the correct response from a–d. Then listen again and give your response.

a   Good, thanks. You?

b   Hiya, and you. It's been ages.

c   Pleased to meet you, Jilly.

d   And you, Mr Robertson.

My review

I can use different phrases for meeting a friend and asking 'how are you?' ❑

I can use different phrases for meeting someone I don't know. ❑

I can use different phrases for introducing someone. ❑

I can ask suitable follow up questions. ❑

---

2 DESCRIBING PEOPLE

Getting started

1 How would you describe the man in this picture?
2 What words would you use to describe yourself?
3 How would other people describe you?

Conversations

07

1 Read and listen to three conversations. Are the people below described in a positive way, a negative way or both? Put a tick (✓) in the correct column(s).

		Positive	Negative
a	Trevor	………	………
b	the woman next to Rosa at work	………	………
c	Rosa's boss	………	………
d	Tanya	………	………
e	Carol	………	………

Conversation 1

Adam: You know Trevor?

Jon: Uh … No, I don't think so.

Adam: Yes, you do. The guy I sometimes play tennis with. And he runs the cafe on Broad Street.

Jon: Oh, yes. He's **kind of tall** and he's got a tattoo. He always wears a dirty leather jacket.

Adam: That's him.

Jon: He **looks a bit odd**. I don't like the look of him.

Adam: Actually, he's **a good laugh**. He's **very intelligent** too. Anyway, he's coming to my party on Friday.

Jon: Oh, OK. Sorry.

Language note

- *Guy* is more common in spoken English than *man*.
- You can also use *guys* to describe a group of people.
- *Guy* and *guys* are very popular in American English.

Conversation 2

Joe: So what's your new job like? Do you like your colleagues?

Rosa: Oh, the job's fine, I suppose, but the people ... They're **a funny bunch**.

Joe: Really? All of them?

Rosa: Yes! They're really strange. The woman I sit next to is **a know-it-all**. Honestly, she thinks she knows everything. it doesn't matter what the topic is, she knows everything about it.

Joe: Oh no.

Rosa: And she's **a name-dropper**. She knows the director of the company, she went to school with this actor, she sat next to this singer on a plane ...

Joe: What about your boss?

Rosa: Terrible. She's a **complete control freak**. She checks my work every day and then changes everything. She tells me to make calls and organise meetings, and then she calls the people and checks the meetings.

Conversation 3

Charlie: See that girl over there?

Dave: Which one?

Charlie: The one with a red bag. She's **kind of short** and **a bit plump**.

Dave: Yes, I see her.

Charlie: That's my brother's new girlfriend, Tanya.

Dave: She's very **smiley**. She looks nice.

Charlie: She looks friendly, yes, but she's so **two-faced**. She says terrible things about people when they can't hear her.

Dave: Oh. That's not nice at all. Who's the woman she's talking to?

Charlie: That's Carol. She's lovely. She **has a heart of gold**. She's a teacher and she helped my brother prepare for his exams last year.

2   Look at the bold words and phrases in the conversations. Add them to the table.

personality		appearance	
1		1	
2		2	
3		3	
4		4	
5		5	
6			
7			
8			

Saying it accurately

1 Complete the sentences with a personal description from Conversations, exercise 2.

A person who ...

1 likes to manage and check everything is a ....

2 is extremely clever is ....

3 uses important people's names to impress others is a ....

4 is extremely kind has ....

5 a strange group of people are ....

6 is fun to be with is a ....

7 says one thing to a person but then says something different, often negative, behind their back is ....

8 believes he/she understands many different topics is a ....

2 Complete the sentences with a physical description similar to the phrases in brackets.

1 She looks .... (*strange*)

2 He's .... (*smiles a lot*)

3 He doesn't do any exercise. He's .... (*not slim*)

4 She's .... (*quite tall*)

5 She's .... (*quite short*)

Saying it clearly

08

1 The schwa sound (ə) is very common in spoken English. Listen and repeat.

09

2 Listen to the phrases below. Pay attention to the weak (unstressed) schwa sounds, highlighted in bold.

1 **a** bit plump

2 **a** name-dropp**er**

3 **a** heart **of** gold

4 kind **of** tall

5 looks **a** bit odd

3 Listen again and repeat. Which three phrases have words that link together?

Saying it appropriately

10

① **Listen to the sentences below and repeat. Pay attention to the stressed (strong) words.**

1 She is a complete control freak. She checks everything.

2 Carol has a heart of gold. She's really kind.

3 Tanya is smiley, but she's two-faced.

4 She's a bit plump.

② **Listen again and underline the stressed (strong) words.**

③ **Rewrite the sentences in exercise 1 to describe someone you know or a character in a TV programme you watch. Then practise saying the sentences and pay attention to the stressed (strong) words in your sentence.**

Useful tip: sounding natural

Using the correct sentence stress and intonation helps you sound natural.

She looks a bit strange.

Get speaking

11

① **Read the following situations and make notes to prepare your responses. Then play the audio and give your answers.**

1 You are talking to your friend at a party and she asks you about a male guest.

• Say his name and then two negative things about him, and explain your opinion.

2 Next she asks you about a female guest, Ana.

• Say two positive things about Ana and explain your opinion.

3 She asks you if you know a group of people.

• Say two negative things about the group and explain your opinion.

4 Then she asks you about another group who she thinks look a little strange.

• Say two positive things about the group and explain your opinion.

② **Close your book and listen to the audio again. Try to give your responses without using your notes.**

My review

I can describe a person's personality.	❏
I can describe a person's appearance.	❏
I can use the schwa sound (ə) correctly.	❏
I can use intonation to express approval and disapproval.	❏

3 TALKING ABOUT THINGS

Getting started

1 What are the men in the photo doing?
2 Where are the men?
3 What do you think is in the boxes?

Conversations

1 Read and listen to the conversations below. Which conversation is about:

a moving flat? ....
b clothes and shopping? ....
c going on holiday? ....

Conversation 1

Penny: What are you wearing to the end-of term party?

Sarah: I'm borrowing my sister's designer dress. It's a long, **sort of** floaty dress.

Penny: Lovely. What colour is it?

Sarah: It's a **greeny** colour. What about you?

Penny: I'm not sure yet. I'm going to that vintage shop this afternoon. It's got **loads of** great **stuff**. Do you want to come?

Sarah: Yeah, OK. My mum bought an old leather coat from there. It looks **kind of** old-fashioned, but it's **pretty** nice.

Language note

We use *borrow* and *lend* when people share objects or possessions.

We use *borrow...* to explain we don't own the object.

*I am **borrowing** a dress from my sister.*

We use *lend...* to explain the object belongs to you, but someone is using it.

*I am **lending** my dress **to** my sister.*

Conversation 2

Ryan: Have you packed everything?

Omar: Yes, I'm ready to go. I'm really excited about moving to the new flat! I can't believe I've got so **many** things. Have you got **much** stuff?

Ryan:	Not really. You've got **hundreds** of boxes here.
Omar:	I know, but I'm not taking everything. I'm going to sell these **things**. They're just old CDs and books. I've got **tonnes** of old books.
Ryan:	And what's this **thing**?
Omar:	It was my grandmother's. It's a **sort of** storage box. It's **pretty** old.
Ryan:	Wow! So what do you use it for?
Omar:	Nothing special. Just **bits and bobs.**

Conversation 3

Celia:	What about this resort? There's **lots of** stuff to do here.
James:	Like what?
Celia:	Organised activities during the day, beach parties or dinners at night, and courses in different water sports.
James:	I don't like that **kind of thing**, to be honest. I'd rather have a quiet holiday and just relax.
Celia:	OK, well, there are **loads of** other websites we can look at. What about this one?
James:	No, I heard some bad **things** about that company.
Celia:	Really? I heard they're **pretty** good.

2   Look at the bold phrases in the conversations. Add them to the table below.

non-precise objects	quantity
1 b...............	8 l............... ....
2 s............... 3 t...............	9 l............... ....
	10 m............... 11 m...............
non-precise descriptions	**exaggerations of quantity**
4 g...............	12 h............... 13 t...............
5 k...............	
6 s...............	
'quite' or 'very'	
7 p...............	

Language note

You can use *stuff* and *things* for objects and belongings as well as activities, but be careful to use the correct grammar:

Countable: *this thing / these things / many things*

Uncountable: *loads of stuff / lots of stuff / much stuff*

Saying it accurately

1 Complete the conversations with the words in the boxes.

borrow	hundreds	many	silvery

1

A: Have you finished the essay? I lost my notes from the lecture and there are **1** ....
things I can't remember.

B: Don't worry. I've got **2** .... of books and notes.

A: Really? Can I **3** .... them, please?

B: Of course. They're in that sort of **4** .... folder on my desk.

kind	stuff	some things	tonnes

2

A: Is it OK if I leave my **1** .... here?

B: Yes, of course You've got **2** .... of bags. What have you bought?

A: Just **3** .... for Helen's party. Did you find a nice birthday present for her?

B: Yeah, I got this. It's a **4** .... of notebook and diary for college.

2 Listen again and check your answers.

Saying it clearly

1 Listen to the phrases below. Pay attention to the words that link together. Is the word in bold strong (stressed) or weak (unstressed)?

1 It's sort_**of** pinky.

2 It's a kind_**of** notebook.

3 You've got loads_**of** bags.

4 There are lots_**of** things to do.

2 Listen again and repeat. Practise linking the words and using the weak pronunciation for *of.*

3 Write four sentences describing things with the words in brackets. Then practise saying the sentences. Pay attention to the words that link together and use the weak pronunciation for *of.*

1 (sort of) ....

2 (kind of) ....

3 (loads of) ....

4 (lots of) ....

Saying it appropriately

1   Read the sentences below. Which words do you think will be stressed?

1   It's pretty old.

2   You've got tonnes of bags.

3   There are hundreds of old books here.

4   I heard they're pretty good.

2   Listen and check. Listen again and repeat. Practise using exaggeration in your sentences.

Useful tip: stressing the right word

Remember to stress the word that shows the exaggeration. This shows your listener which words are the most important.

---

3   Read and listen to the non-precise descriptions below. Which speaker sounds uncertain? Put a tick (✓) in the correct column.

	1	2
1 It's a greeny colour.	....	....
2 It's a sort of storage box.	....	....
3 It's a bluey colour.	....	....
4 It's a kind of notebook.	....	....

4   Listen to the sentences in exercise 3 again. This time the speakers all sound uncertain. Listen again and repeat. Practise using the uncertain tone.

Useful tip: using uncertain intonation

When you are giving a non-precise description, you can use uncertain intonation to show you know you are not completely sure about the thing you are describing.

Get speaking

1   You are going to listen to five questions about things you own. First, listen and make notes on your answers. Then listen again and give your answers.

My review

I can talk about things with non-precise descriptions.	❏
I can use correct pronunciation and link words together.	❏
I can use correct stress to show exaggeration in descriptions.	❏
I can use uncertain intonation for non-precise descriptions.	❏

---

4 TALKING ABOUT PLACES

Getting started

1 Where are these people?

2 What are they doing?

3 What are they saying?

Conversations

19

1 Read and listen to the conversations. Which conversations are describing how to find a place and which conversations are describing places?

how to find a place: ....

describing places: ....

Conversation 1

Bob: Do you know where we can get a taxi?

Carlo: Yeah, down there. See the cafe on the corner? There's a taxi rank opposite. You can't miss it.

Conversation 2

Dan: You should go to New York for your holiday.

Tim: Really? Isn't it very noisy and unsafe?

Dan: No, not at all. When we were there, we stayed in a beautiful hotel. You know the Empire State building?

Tim: The really high skyscraper?

Dan: Yes, we stayed a couple of blocks from there.

Tim: Mmm, sounds good.

Dan: Yes, we did loads of stuff. Went to art galleries... they were packed! The shops ... they were amazing! It was the best holiday.

Useful tip: spoken questions

Spoken questions like *See the cafe on the corner?* are usually different to written questions, like *Can you see the cafe on the corner?* They use fewer words and simpler grammar.

Conversation 3

Lorna: How was your trip?

Anne: Terrible. It was the worst weekend.

Lorna: Oh no, what happened?

Anne: Everything went wrong. We got to the hotel and it was closed and empty. So, we went to another hotel ... it was really noisy; we went out to a restaurant in the evening; it was disgusting! It was just terrible.

Conversation 4

Sam: I'm looking for Mr Kay's office.

Vicky: Sure. You know where the big meeting room is? Go past that and it's on the left.

Useful tip: adding a pause

Remember to use a pause when asking questions during a conversation, even if you don't need a reply. This gives the other person time to think and reply.

You know where the big meeting room is? [PAUSE] *Go past that and it's on the left.*

Conversation 5

Bella: Excuse me, is there a good restaurant round here?

Meg: Yes, there's a great Italian restaurant about five minutes from here. Go up this hill and when you see a small bookshop, turn sharp right and it's behind there.

2 Read and listen to the conversations again.

1 Which three places do the people want to find?

....

....

....

2 Underline positive and negative adjectives to describe places.

3 Look back at the conversations. Find and underline three more questions in the short spoken form.

Example: ~~Do you~~ See the cafe on the corner?

Saying it accurately

1 These questions are in the short spoken form. Rewrite the questions into the longer written form using the words and phrases below.

Can you	Do (x 2)	Is that

1 See the cafe on the corner? ....

2 You know the Empire State building? ....

3 The really high skyscraper? ....

4 You know where the big meeting room is? ....

2 Rewrite these written questions as shorter spoken questions.

1 Is that the big park in the centre of town?...

2 Do you know Trafalgar Square?..

3 Do you know where the canteen is?...

4 Can you see the park at the end of the street?...

3 Listen and check your answers. Listen again and repeat.

20

> **Useful tip: rising intonation**
>
> Speakers usually use rising intonation at the end of questions. Rising intonation means that your voice goes up as you move through the word or phrase.

Saying it clearly

1 Listen to the descriptions. Notice how the speaker pauses (***) and then the voice falls towards the adjective. Listen again and repeat.

21

> We went to the museums, *** which were boring; the art galleries, *** they were packed; the city centre, *** it was dirty; the restaurants, *** they were expensive.

> **Useful tip: falling intonation**
>
> Speakers usually use falling intonation on the adjective at the end of a phrase. Falling intonation means that your voice goes down towards the end of a phrase.

Saying it appropriately

1 Listen to the sentences below and tick (✓) if the intonation is correct. Questions 1–3 should rise at the end. Phrases 4–6 should fall on the adjective.

1 See the train station? ....

2 You know where Mike's office is? ....

3 You know the old Post Office building? ....

4 We went to the parks, which were boring. ....

5 We went on some bus tours, which were brilliant. ....

6 We visited the art galleries, which were beautiful. ....

2 Now listen to the correct intonation of the sentences in exercise 1. Listen and repeat.

Get speaking

1 Listen to someone asking you for directions to the places below. Make notes on the directions (use your imagination or use examples from the unit) and include one short spoken question.

1 the reception desk

> **Audio:** Excuse me, I'm looking for the reception desk.
>
> **You:** You know where the stairs are? Go down the stairs and the reception desk is at the front of the building.

2 the train station

3 a good cafe

2 Listen again and try to answer without using your notes.

3 Think of a place you have visited and write a description about it with four adjectives. Use the description in Saying it clearly, exercise 1 to help you. Practise saying your sentences and using a pause and then falling intonation on the adjective.

....

....

My review

I can give directions.	❏
I can talk about places.	❏
I can use correct intonation in questions.	❏
I can use correct intonation to describe places.	❏

5 MAKING ARRANGEMENTS

Getting started

1 How do you make arrangements with friends, family and colleagues? Choose an option below.

by social media   by phone   by text   in person

2 What do you usually say when making arrangements?

Conversations

25

1 Read and listen to the four conversations. Match each conversation with a description below. There is one extra description.

a changing an arrangement ....

b colleagues making an arrangement ....

c friends making an arrangement ....

d postponing an arrangement ....

Conversation 1

Sarah: Hello?

Clare: Hi, Sarah, it's Clare. How are you?

Sarah: Oh, hiya! Not bad, thanks. You?

Clare: Fine, thanks. I'm waiting for the bus, so I thought I'd give you a quick ring. How did your interview go?

Sarah: Actually, it went really well. They offered me the job!

Clare: Oh, brilliant! We should celebrate. **Fancy coming round for dinner tonight? Let's say 7 p.m.?**

Sarah: OK.

Clare: **Great, see you later.** Bye.

Sarah: Bye.

Useful tip: prepositions

When making arrangements, learn to use prepositions correctly. Keep a record of prepositions and the words that go before or after.

*I'll meet you **at** 10 a.m. Fancy going **for** a walk tomorrow?*

Conversation 2

Lisa: Hi Sue, **is it still OK for you to pick me up tomorrow?**

Sue: **Yes, no problem.**

Lisa: **Is 5.30 OK?** The traffic can be bad at that time.

Sue: Yeah, good point. **I'll pick you up at 5 p.m., then.**

Lisa: OK. **See you then.** Bye.

Sue: Bye.

Conversation 3

Steven: Hello, Steven speaking.

Richard: Hi, Steven, it's Richard. I'm just phoning to finalise dates for the board meeting. **Would you be able to attend on Friday or Monday?**

Steven: OK, let me check my diary ... I can make Friday anytime or Monday afternoon. How does that sound?

Richard: Great. **Shall we say Friday at 10 a.m.,** then?

Steven: **Yes, that's fine.**

Richard: Thanks, Steven. I'll email you directions and details now. **Look forward to seeing you then.**

Steven: And you. Thanks. Bye.

Richard: Bye.

Conversation 4

Paul: **Are you still free for lunch today?**

Heidi: Actually, I'm really busy. **I'm running late. Can we make it tomorrow?**

Paul: Sure. Same place?

Heidi: Great. Thanks, Paul. **See you tomorrow.**

Paul: Bye.

2   Look at the three stages of making an arrangement below. Read and listen to the conversations again. Complete the table with the bold phrases from each conversation.

	1	2	3	4
arrangement	Fancy coming round for dinner tonight?			
time	Let's say 7 p.m.?			
response	Great, see you later.			

Language note

Use *still* to check that your arrangement has not changed.
*Is it **still** OK for you to pick me up tomorrow?*

3 Look at your answers to exercise 2. Which conversation is formal? Underline the examples of formal language.

Useful tip: formal and informal language

Remember to change your language between formal and informal. Use informal language with friends and people you know well. Use formal language in professional situations and with people you don't know.

Saying it accurately

1 Complete the sentences with the prepositions below.

at	for (x 2)	on	to (x 2)	up

1 Fancy going .... a coffee later?

2 Is it still OK for you .... pick me up from work?

3 Would you be able to attend the meeting .... Wednesday morning?

4 Shall we say tomorrow .... about 9 a.m.?

5 Look forward .... seeing you.

6 I'll pick you .... in half an hour.

7 Are you still free .... tennis tomorrow?

Language note

Use *Fancy + -ing* to make arrangements with a friend.
***Fancy coming** round for dinner?* (NOT ***Fancy to come** round for dinner?*)

2 Match 1–4 to a–d to make questions.

1 Can we		**a**	7 p.m.
2 Is		**b**	make it tomorrow
3 Let's say		**c**	say Friday at 8 a.m.
4 Shall we		**d**	7.30 OK?

Saying it appropriately

 Read the responses below. Think about the way a speaker would give the response. Would they sound enthusiastic?

1 Great, see you later.

2 Yes, no problem.

3 Yes, that's fine.

4 Look forward to seeing you then.

5 I'm running late. Can we make it tomorrow?

 Listen and check. In which response does the speaker sound sorry?

3 Listen again and repeat each response.

Get speaking

 You are going to call a friend to make an arrangement. Prepare your conversation by making notes on the stages below.

1 check your friend can still pick you up

2 confirm the time

3 give your response

Useful tip: sounding sorry or enthusiastic

Remember to sound sorry or to sound enthusiastic when you give your response. The way you speak (your intonation) is as important as the words you say.

 Now start the conversation. Ask your fi rst question. Then play the audio and listen to the response. Then continue with the conversation.

You: *Is it still OK for you to pick me up?*

Your friend (audio): *Hi. Yes, what time shall I pick you up?*

3 This time your friend calls you to check an arrangement. Listen and give your response when you hear the beep. Pause the audio if necessary.

1 apologise and explain why you need to change the arrangement

2 give your thanks and give your response

 Now you receive a call from a colleague. Respond to the questions. Use your answers in Conversations, exercise 2 to help you.

My review

I can make a formal or informal arrangement.	❑
I can postpone an arrangement.	❑
I can change an arrangement.	❑
I can sound sorry and sound enthusiastic in my responses.	❑

---

6 MAKING REQUESTS

Getting started

1 Where are these people?
2 Who is making a request?
3 What do you think is the request?

Conversations

 1 Read the questions below. Think about where you would hear these questions.

- Excuse me, would you mind taking our photo please?
- Do you mind if I hand in the essay on Monday?
- Could you move your coat please?
- Is it OK if I go to the cinema with Cathy tonight?
- Sorry, could you possibly explain that again please?
- Excuse me, is it OK if I park my car here?

30

2 Read and listen to the conversations. Do you think your ideas in exercise 1 were correct?

Conversation 1

A: **Excuse me, would you mind** taking our photo please?

B: Of course. Ready? Smile!

A: Thank you.

Conversation 2

A: **Do you mind if I** hand in the essay on Monday?

B: Well, I'll need it in the morning. Is that possible?

A: Yes, I can give it to you before 10 a.m.

B: That's fine, then. Thank you for letting me know.

Conversation 3

A: **Is it OK if I** go to the cinema with Cathy tonight?

B: OK, but you must be home by 10.30.

Conversation 4

A: **Can I** use your mobile, Mark?

B: Yeah, it's in my bag.

A: Thanks.

Conversation 5

A: **Could you possibly** explain that again, please?

B: Of course. Complete form T7H89, then go online and enter the code from your registration pack and complete the online application.

Conversation 6

A: **Could you** move your coat please? This seat is reserved for me.

B: I suppose so.

A: Thank you.

Conversation 7

A: **Excuse me, is it OK if I** park my car here?

B: Actually, that's the manager's space. You can park over there.

A: Oh right. OK, thanks for your help.

Language note

Use **indirect questions** in formal situations, to be polite to people you don't know.

Sorry, could you possibly explain that again, please?

Use **direct questions** in informal situations, with friends and people you know.

Can I use your mobile?

③ Look at the conversations again. Do the people know each other? Decide which type of question is asked in each of the conversations above.

1 *indirect*   **4** ....   **7** ....

2 ....   **5** ....

3 ....   **6** ....

4 Look at the bold questions in the conversations. Some are formal and some are informal. Add the questions under the correct heading below.

formal

1 Excuse me, would you mind taking our photo, please?

2 ....

3 ....

4 ....

5 ....

informal

1 ....

2 ....

Saying it accurately

1 Complete the questions with the words below.

can	if	mind	OK	possibly	you

1 Sorry, could you .... tell me where the train station is please?

2 .... I leave my things here?

3 Do you mind .... I come to class a bit late tomorrow?

4 Could .... pick me up tonight?

5 Excuse me, is it .... if I use your printer?

6 Excuse me, would you .... helping me with this suitcase?

2 Correct the verb forms underlined in the questions below.

1 Would you mind <u>help</u> me with this bag?

2 Could you <u>giving</u> this to Joe?

3 Could you possibly <u>telling</u> me where the train station is please?

4 Is it OK if <u>I'm calling</u> you later?

5 Could you <u>passing</u> me that book please?

6 Do you mind if I <u>paying</u> you later?

7 Can I <u>using</u> your Wi-Fi?

Saying it clearly

31

1 Listen carefully to the questions below. Underline the stressed words.

1 Excuse me, would you mind taking our photo?

2 Could you possibly explain that again please?

3 Do you mind if I hand in the essay on Monday?

4 Is it OK if I go to the cinema tonight?

5 Can I use your mobile?

6 Could you move your coat, please?

2 Listen again and repeat.

Saying it appropriately

1 Listen to the questions below. Which speakers sound polite and which sound impolite? Put a tick (✓) in the correct column.

		Polite	Impolite
1	Excuse me, would you mind moving your suitcase?	....	....
2	Could you possibly say that again, please?	....	....
3	Do you mind if I miss school tomorrow?	....	....
4	Excuse me, is it ok if I borrow your phone?	....	....
5	Could you email me later?	....	....
6	Can I have another coffee?	....	....

2 Now listen to the polite questions. Pay attention to the rising intonation (the way the speaker's voice rises towards the end of the question). Rising intonation makes the questions sound more polite. Listen and repeat.

3 Record yourself asking the questions in exercise 1. Listen to your recording. Do you sound polite?

Get speaking

1 You're going to make requests to the people below about situations 1–6. Think about what type of question you should use. Make notes if you like.

	people	request
1	parents	you want to visit a friend tonight
2	stranger	you want to sit at their table in a cafe
3	friend	you want to borrow his book
4	stranger on a bus	his bag is on your seat
5	receptionist	you want her to explain something difficult about an application form
6	teacher	you want to hand in your homework next week, not this week

2 Now play the audio. After each beep, you should speak. Then listen to their response.

My review

I can use direct question with people I know.	❏
I can use indirect questions with people I don't know.	❏
I can use correct sentence stress in questions.	❏
I can sound polite when I ask direct and indirect questions.	❏

7 ORDERING AND BUYING

Getting started

1 Where are these people?
2 What is the woman buying?
3 What do you think the people are saying?

Conversations

35

Read and listen to the conversations. In which conversation does the person not pay for something? ....

Conversation 1

Gina:	**I'd like to reserve** a place on next month's English course please.
Receptionist:	Of course. Is it the morning or the afternoon course?
Gina:	Oh. **How much does** each one **cost**?
Receptionist:	The morning course is £400 per week and the afternoon is £350. And the afternoon course also has a free conversation class on Fridays.
Gina:	**That sounds good. Can I have a** place on the afternoon course, then?
Receptionist:	OK. Now, you can pay in full now. Or you can leave a deposit today and pay the rest on the first day.
Gina:	Great. **I'll pay now, please.**

Conversation 2

John:	**Could I book** a table for dinner tonight, please?
Waiter:	Yes, of course. How many people?
John:	Four.
Waiter:	And what time? We have tables at 6.30 or 9 p.m.
John:	**Let me think.** 6.30 is better, please.
Waiter:	OK, and what's the name?
John:	Anderson.
Waiter:	Thank you. So that's a table for four people, at 6.30p.m. tonight.
John:	Great. Thanks for your help. Bye.

Conversation 3

Pat:	Hello. **Do you have any** tickets left for the concert tonight?
Clerk:	Hmmm, let me check. Yes, there are a few tickets.
Pat:	Brilliant. How much are they?
Clerk:	The best seats are £85 each.
Pat:	**That's very expensive.** Are there any cheaper ones?
Clerk:	We have two at £60. They're near the back of the stadium.
Pat:	That's fine. **I'll take those, please.**
Clerk:	Certainly. That's £120 please.
Pat:	**Here you are.**
Clerk:	Thank you. Enter your PIN when you're ready. ... Thank you. Here's your receipt and here are your tickets. Doors open at 7:45 p.m. Have a good night!
Pat:	Thank you.

Conversation 4

Barista:	Hello, what can I get you?
Deb:	Hi, **can I get** a black coffee, please?
Barista:	To have in or take away?
Deb:	To go, please.
Barista:	Anything else? Any sandwiches or pastries?
Deb:	**Let me see.** I'll have a chocolate cookie, please.
Barista:	OK.

2 Read and listen to the conversations again. Put a tick (✓) in the correct column.

	True	False
1 Gino books a place on the morning course.	....	....
2 The conversation class is free.	....	....
3 Andy wants to book a table for dinner.	....	....
4 He chooses a table at 9 p.m.	....	....
5 Pat buys two tickets for the concert.	....	....
6 She pays by cash.	....	....
7 Deb's conversation is in a cafe.	....	....
8 She orders a sandwich.	....	....

3 Look at the bold phrases in the conversations. Answer the questions below.

1 Which six phrases or questions show the speaker making an enquiry?

....

....

2 Which two phrases show the speaker thinking about the decision?

....

3 Which two phrases show the speaker's opinion about the price?

....

4 Which two phrases show the speaker making a decision?

....

Saying it accurately

1 Number the lines in the correct order to make a conversation.

a Yes, how many would you like? ....

b That's very expensive. ....

c Thank you. ....

d Well, we do have standing tickets. They're only £20 each. ....

e Four please. How much are they? ....

f Do you have any tickets for PopFest? ....

g That sounds good. I'll take those please. ....

h They're £50 for the VIP seats. ....

i OK. That's £80 please. Thank you. And here are your tickets. ....

2 Listen and check.

36

Saying it clearly

37

1 Listen to four different speakers. Circle the prices you hear. There are two extra prices.

1 £4.15   **3** £20   **5** £50

2 £4.50   **4** 20p   **6** £100

38

2 How many different ways can you say the prices below? Listen and check your ideas.

1 £6.15   **2** £80   **3** £100   **4** £7.50

Useful tip: vocabulary for money

£2,500.00 = *two and a half thousand pounds* ✓

£2.50 = *two and a half pounds* ✗

You can say *50p* (say *pee*) or *50 pence*.

In British English, people often say *quid* (not *pounds*) when talking to friends.

3 Listen again and repeat.

4 How many different ways can you say these times? Listen and check your ideas.

1 7.45 **2** 6.30 **3** 9

Saying it appropriately

1 Listen carefully to the sentences below. Use a comma to mark the position in the sentences where the speaker pauses. Listen again and repeat.

1 Let me see OK that sounds good. **2** Let me think I'll take those please.

2 Now listen to how the underlined words in these sentences link together.

1 <u>Do you</u> h<u>ave any t</u>ickets for tonight's fi lm?

2 <u>Can I</u> get two teas to go, please?

3 <u>Could I</u> book a place on the course, please?

3 Listen and repeat. Practise linking your words together.

Get speaking

1 You are going to have three conversations where you reserve or buy something. Read the notes below to help you prepare. Then play the audio and give your responses.

1 You phone the college to ask about English courses.
  • First, say you would like a place on the next course.
  • Then ask how much it costs.
  • Say the price sounds good, and pay for your place now.

2 You go to a ticket booth to get tickets for tonight's concert.
  • First, ask if there are any tickets.
  • Then ask how much they cost.
  • Say that the first price is too expensive, and buy three cheaper ones.

3 You visit a cafe. The server speaks first, so answer his questions.
  • Order a drink.
  • Then order something to eat.
  • Choose if you want to have it in or take away.

My review

I can use suitable phrases for ordering and buying things. ❏

I can say numbers and times clearly. ❏

I can use pauses and link words correctly to sound natural. ❏

8 SPEAKING ON THE PHONE

Getting started

1 Do you use your mobile, Skype or a landline (the phone in your home) to make calls?

2 Do you think it's rude to use a mobile when you are out with friends?

Conversations

43

Read and listen to the three conversations. Answer the questions below.

a Who wants to arrange another time to meet his friend? ....

b Who has a problem with her mobile? ....

c Who refuses an offer three times? ....

d Which conversation is informal? ....

Conversation 1

Sandra: Hi, this is Sandra. **Sorry I can't take your call**. Leave your name and number, and **I'll get back to you as soon as I can**.

Dan: Hey Sandra, how's things? It's Dan. **I'm just calling to say** I can't meet you tonight, I'm sorry. I have to work late. Call me when you get this message, then we can arrange when to meet up. OK? Bye.

Conversation 2

Receptionist: Hello, Tony's Salon.

Lisa: Hello, I'd like to book a haircut for tomorrow.

Receptionist: Sorry, **the line's terrible. Can you repeat that?**

Lisa: Can you hear me now? Hello? I'd like to book a haircut tomorrow.

Receptionist: That's better. Yes, we have one appointment at 11.45. What's your name please?

Lisa: Great. It's Lisa Evans.

Receptionist: Sorry, **I didn't catch that**.

Lisa: Lisa Evans. Sorry, the reception's bad on my mobile.

| Receptionist: | Yes, it's difficult to hear you. We'll see you tomorrow Lisa. Bye for now. |
| Lisa: | Bye. |

Conversation 3

Sheree:	Good evening, can I speak to Mr Dawson?
Mr Dawson:	**Yes, speaking.**
Sheree:	Good evening Mr Dawson. My name's Sheree and I'm calling from Web World, your internet provider. I'm phoning tonight to tell you about the offer on the gold contract and this is one—
Mr Dawson:	Thanks, but I don't want to change contract.
Sheree:	Mr Dawson, you can save money with the gold package. You need to make a one-off payment of—
Mr Dawson:	No, I'm sorry, I'm really not interested.
Sheree:	I don't want you to miss a great opportunity and I really think—
Mr Dawson:	**Listen, I'm not interested.** Now, thank you for calling, but my answer is no. Goodbye.

2 Look at the bold phrases in the conversations and match them to the meanings below.

1 I can't answer the phone. ....

2 I'll call you back. ....

3 I'm phoning because... ....

4 There is a problem with the phone. ....

5 Say that again. ....

6 I didn't hear that. ....

7 Yes, that's me. ....

8 Pay attention. I am not interested. ....

Saying it accurately

1 **Read the sentences and choose the correct word.**

1 Hi, this is Sylvia. Sorry I can't *leave / take* your call.

2 I'll *get / phone* back to you.

3 Call me when you *get / reply* this message.

4 Can I *call / speak* to Mrs Plant?

5 *Listen / Speak*, I'm not interested.

6 Can you *hear / listen* me now?

7 Sorry, I didn't *catch / listen* that.

8 The *line / phone* is terrible.

2 Listen and check your answers.

Saying it clearly

1 Listen to two speakers reading the voicemail message below. Which speaker is clear and easy to understand? What is the problem with the other speaker?

> Hi Steve, it's Jon here. Just calling to say I can come to your party next week. But is it Friday or Saturday? Give me a call when you get this message, OK? Bye.

....

....

2 Read and listen to the good speaker. Then listen again and say the words at the same time as the speaker. Try to speak at the same pace and leave the same pauses.

3 Complete the voicemail message below with your own ideas. Then practise saying the message. If possible, use your phone to make a 'real' call.

> Hi ...., it's .... here. Just calling to say I ....
> ....? Give me a call when you get this message. OK? Bye.

Saying it appropriately

1 Read and listen to an extract from Conversation 3. Try to complete the gaps with the sounds you hear.

Sheree:	I'm phoning tonight to tell you about the offer on the gold contract and this—
Mr Dawson:	1 ...., Thank you, but I, 2 ...., don't want to change contract.
Sheree:	Mr Dawson, you can save money with the gold package. You need to make a one-off payment of—
Mr Dawson:	3 ...., No, I'm sorry, I'm really not interested.
Sheree:	I don't want you to miss a great opportunity and I really think—
Mr Dawson:	4 .... Listen, I'm not interested. Now thank you for calling, but my answer is no. Goodbye.

Useful tip: using sounds to express yourself

Being an effective speaker means using suitable sounds to express your feelings. For example, er, um, mmm for uncertainty, and a sigh when you are upset or angry. These sounds are very useful when you are speaking on the phone.

48

Listen and repeat Mr Dawson's lines. Think about how Mr Dawson is feeling.

Get speaking

49

Read the following situations and make notes to prepare what you are going to say. Then play the audio and speak when you hear the beep.

1   You phone your friend, but your call goes to her voicemail.

- leave a message and say that you want to meet
- ask which day is OK for your friend
- ask her to call you back

2   Your friend calls you but she says the reception is bad.

- agree and say you can't hear
- ask her to repeat what she said
- suggest a time to meet and say bye

3   You receive a phone call from a mobile phone company.

- make uncertain noises and try to say no
- make uncertain noises and try to say no again
- sigh and say no clearly, then say bye

Useful tip: speaking at a natural pace

An important speaking skill is the ability to speak clearly and at a natural pace – not fast and not slow. This helps you to improve your fluency and it helps people understand you.

My review

I can have formal and informal conversations on the phone.	❏
I can leave a voicemail.	❏
I can speak clearly and at a natural pace.	❏
I can use suitable noises to show uncertainty or that I am upset.	❏

9 SHOWING INTEREST IN A CONVERSATION

Getting started

1 How easy do you find it to start and to end a conversation?
2 Do you like talking to new people?
3 What topics do you enjoy talking about with friends?

Conversations

50

Read and listen to the conversations below. Each conversation includes someone giving some news. In which conversations are the people not interested in developing a conversation? ....

Conversation 1

June:	Excuse me, does this bus go to the Royal Hospital?
Nicola:	Yes, it does.
June:	Oh good, thanks. Can I sit here? My sister's in hospital. I'm going to visit her.
Nicola:	Mmm.
June:	It's nothing serious. Just a small operation. She'll be out tomorrow.
Nicola:	Right.
June:	Yes, my husband's going to finish work early and then we're going to collect her. She's going to stay with us for about—
Nicola:	This is my stop. **Sorry, I have to go.**

Conversation 2

Harry:	Hi Tony, guess who I saw last night.
Tony:	Who? Not Geoff?
Harry:	No, Mr Simpson. You know, our old history teacher.
Tony:	**Really? So** what was he saying?
Harry:	Nothing really. He remembered our class. He still lives near the school, but he's going to emigrate to Canada next year.
Tony:	**No way!** He was such a nice teacher, wasn't he?
Harry:	Yeah, always happy. Anyway, then he started saying—
Tony:	Listen, sorry Harry. **I'm in a rush. I have to be at** the doctor's at 11. Can I call you later?

Conversation 3

Tina: Guess what? I've got two offers for jobs when I graduate!

Diane: **Really?** Well done. What are they?

Tina: One is with a financial firm in the city. They only take two graduates each year and I'm one!

Diane: **No way!** That's great. What's the other one?

Tina: It's working as a volunteer in Africa.

Diane: **Wow!** They both sound amazing!

Conversation 4

Sam: I'm glad I caught you, Ella. Have you got a minute?

Ella: Not really. **I'd love to chat but I have to** leave early tonight.

Sam: Oh, where are you going?

Ella: Back to my parents' for the weekend. **Sorry. I better get going.**

Sam: Oh, that's a shame. I'm having a party tomorrow night and—

Ella: Sorry, Sam, **I really have to go.** I'm catching a train at half past.

Useful tip: responding in a conversation

Your responses in a conversation change how it develops. For example, give one or two word responses when you'd like the conversation to end. *Right.*

Ask short questions or make short exclamations when you're interested in developing the conversation. *Really? No way!*

Language note

A polite way to show that you want to end a conversation is to say 'I better get going'. *I better get going = I should leave*

2 Underline four questions in Conversation 2 which show Tony is interested in the news.

3 Underline three questions or exclamations in Conversation 3 which show Diane is interested in the news.

4 Put the bold words and phrases from the conversations in the categories below.

Questions/Exclamations	Phrases to conclude a conversation
....	....
....	....
....	....
	....
	....

Saying it accurately

1 Complete the sentences with the words in the box below.

better	really	rush	way

1 No ....! That's great news!

2 I'm in a .... I have to be at the dentist at 10.

3 I .... have to go. I'm meeting a friend in ten minutes.

4 Sorry, I .... get going.

2 Put the lines in the correct order to make a dialogue.

1 One is here in London. They gave me a scholarship too!

2 In America at the same university my sister goes to..

3 Guess what? I've got a place at two universities!

4 No way! That's great. Where's the other one?

5 Wow! Well done. Which ones?

Saying it clearly

1 Read the sentences below. Can you understand the meaning of the sentences with the gaps? What do you think are the missing words?

1 I have .... go.

2 I'm in .... rush.

3 I have .... be .... doctor's at 10.

4 I'd love .... chat but I have .... go.

Useful tip: sentence stress

The important words in a sentence are stressed because they show the meaning of the sentence. The less important words are unstressed.

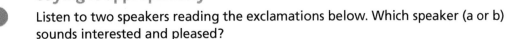

Listen and complete the gaps. Then listen again and repeat. Try to use correct sentence stress.

Saying it appropriately

Listen to two speakers reading the exclamations below. Which speaker (a or b) sounds interested and pleased?

1 Really?   **2** No way!   **3** Wow!

Now listen and repeat the correct intonation.

Listen to the phrases below and mark where the speaker pauses. Then listen again and repeat. Practise using pauses.

1 Sorry, I'm afraid I have to go.   **2** Listen, sorry Harry. I'm in a rush.

3 Sorry. I better get going.

Useful tip: using pauses

Use a pause before or after you say *sorry*. This makes the person you're talking to listen carefully to what you're saying.

Get speaking

Read the following situations and make notes to prepare your responses. Then play the audio and give your responses.

1 A woman sits next to you on the bus and starts talking to you.

- Give two responses to show you are not interested and then conclude the conversation.

2 A friend is telling you about some good news she has.

- Make three exclamations to show you're interested.

3 A colleague wants to talk to you, but you have to leave for an appointment.

- Make an apology and use a phrase to conclude the conversation.

My review

I can react to a speaker and make exclamations to sound interested. ☐

I can react to a speaker and conclude the conversation. ☐

I can use interested intonation. ☐

I can use pauses correctly. ☐

10 DEVELOPING A CONVERSATION

Getting started

1 Where are the people?
2 What do you think the conversation is about?
3 What topics do people talk about at work?

Conversations

56

1 Read and listen to the conversations. Match the descriptions of the people with the conversations.

a colleagues at work ....
b flatmates at home ....
c students studying overseas ....
d tourists on holiday ....

Conversation 1

Ann: I **really liked** the tour. I'm glad we chose that one.

Matt: Me too. I **loved** it. What a great weekend!

Ann: The tour guide was **good**.

Matt: **Really good. And knowledgeable too.**

Ann: Mmm. What I didn't like was the cable car ride. That was **scary**.

Matt: Yeah, I know what you mean. It was **horrible** when it moved quickly.

Useful tip: developing a conversation

(1) The first speaker makes a comment.

(2) The second speaker agrees and repeats the comment using 'stronger' words.

(3) The second speaker often adds an additional comment or point on the topic.

Conversation 2

Jen: I don't really like studying here.

Karen: No, me neither.

Jen:	I miss my family. It's **very hard** living away from home.
Karen:	**Very difficult. I feel homesick too.**
Jen:	The weather is **bad**, isn't it?
Karen:	**Terrible. It's really cold.**
Jen:	What I do **like** is meeting new people. Do you know what I mean?
Karen:	Yeah, me too. **I've got loads of new friends now.**

Conversation 3

Will:	Wow! What a **great** seminar!
Gary:	**Amazing! I can't wait to start the project.**
Will:	Me too. They're such a **nice** bunch of people too.
Gary:	**Really nice. And very enthusiastic.**
Will:	I think the company is **better** now that new guy is in charge.
Gary:	You mean Claude? Yeah, it's made **a big difference**.

Conversation 4

Max:	Thanks for cooking dinner, Sarah. It was **lovely**.
Rosa:	Yeah, thanks Sarah. It was **delicious**.
Sarah:	Oh, thanks. I'm pleased you liked it. So what are you cooking me tomorrow night?
Max:	Maybe curry? Do you like that?
Sarah:	Not really. **I'm not keen on** spicy food.
Rosa:	Me neither. I don't like spicy food at all. **Why don't we go out for pizza instead?**
Max:	OK. I'll book Gino's.
Sarah:	Great idea!

2 Read and listen to the conversations again. Complete the table below to show how the topic of a conversation develops.

	topic	first speaker	second speaker	additional point
1	tour guide	good	**1**	And knowledgeable too.
	cable car ride	scary	**2**	
2	studying	**3**	Very difficult.	**4** ....
	weather	bad	**5**	It's really cold.
	meeting new people	like	Me too.	I've got loads of new friends now.

topic	first speaker	second speaker	additional point
3	seminar	6...................	amazing	I can't wait to start the project.
	people	7...................	really nice	8...
	the company	better	big difference	
4	dinner	lovely	9..................	
	curry	I'm not keen on spicy food.	I don't like spicy food at all.	Why don't we go for pizza instead?

Saying it accurately

1 Read the extracts from conversations below. Complete the gaps with words from the box.

> difficult　　　like　　　neither　　　really　　　terrible　　　too

1 **A:** That was a great film. I really enjoyed it.

 B: Me .... It was really exciting.

2 **A:** It's very hard revising for exams.

 B: Mmm, very .... My sister gives me extra tuition.

3 **A:** I didn't really enjoy the trip.

 B: No, me .... It was pretty boring.

4 **A:** Our classmates are so nice, aren't they?

 B: Mmmmm, ... nice. And very clever.

5 **A:** I didn't .... that restaurant.

 B: No, I hated it. The waiters were very rude.

6 **A:** The course is bad, isn't it?

 B: .... The seminars are so boring.

2 Listen and check.

57

Saying it clearly

1 Say the words below out loud. Think about how many syllables (different parts of the word) there are in each word.

> amazing　　　difficult　　　exciting　　　friendly　　　handsome
> interesting　　　seminar　　　terrible　　　knowledgeable

2   Add the words in exercise 1 next to the correct stress pattern below.

O o   *friendly*   ....

O o o   *difficult*   ....

o O o   ....

O o o o   ....

3   Listen and check your answers. Listen again and repeat.

58

Saying it appropriately

1   Read and listen to the responses below. Pay attention to the underlined stressed words.

59

1   **A:** This band is <u>good</u>!

    B: <u>Really</u> good. And very <u>loud</u> too!

2   **A:** I <u>don't like</u> getting the bus.

    B: Me <u>neither</u>. It's <u>dirty</u> and <u>noisy</u>.

3   **A:** I <u>love</u> my new car. It's <u>great</u>, isn't it?

    B: <u>Amazing</u>. It's <u>fast</u> too.

2   Listen again and repeat.

Get speaking

1   First, read the following situations. Then listen to the audio and make notes to help you prepare your responses. Then play the audio again and give your responses.

60

1   You are talking with a friend about a trip you took together. Neither of you enjoyed it.

   • Respond by agreeing with your friend's three opinions.

2   You are discussing a training course you attended with a colleague.

   • Respond to your colleague's three positive opinions.

2   Close your book and listen to the audio again. Try to give your responses without using your notes.

My review

I can develop a conversation and add an additional point.   ❏

I can use *Me too* and *Me neither* correctly.   ❏

I can give correct sentence stress in the repeated comment.   ❏

I can correctly use syllables and word stress.   ❏

11 CHECKING FOR UNDERSTANDING

Getting started

1 How often do you not understand something in a conversation?
2 How do you feel when that happens?
3 What do you say or do when that happens?

Conversations

61

Read and listen to the four conversations below. Match the topics below with the conversations.

a a changed decision about an arrangement ....
b a mistake at work ....
c a problem with a computer ....
d an organised student ....

Conversation 1

Beth: So did you call Pete about confirming the delivery?

Tracy: **You mean** the date of the delivery?

Beth: Yes. And then you need to enter the delivery date into the spreadsheet. Here. **See what I mean?**

Tracy: Oh yeah, thanks.

Beth: I forgot to do that last month and the boss went crazy!

Tracy: **What do you mean?**

Beth: She was really angry. She was shouting at me and screaming, **you know**. She was horrible to me.

Tracy: Well, a silly mistake can cost a company lots of money.

Beth: **What are you saying?**

Tracy: Nothing. **What I'm trying to say is** you made a little mistake, but it meant the company lost money. That's why the boss was really angry.

Conversation 2

Alan: Mr Smith, can you help me with this new software?

Mr Smith: Yeah, of course. Just click on the blue button to start. Then go into the main menu and select 'register'. **Does that make sense?**

Alan:	OK, I click on the blue button, select 'register' and then it starts. **Is that right?**
Mr Smith:	No, sorry. Let me start again. Click the blue button to start, go into the main menu and *then* select register.
Alan:	OK, **got it!** Thanks.

Useful tip: asking someone to explain

If you don't understand what someone says, ask them to explain it.
What do you mean?

If someone says something that upsets you, you can ask them to explain it using a more aggressive question.
What are you saying?

Conversation 3

Kate:	It's really difficult to find a good student flat, isn't it? It makes me feel so stressed. **Know what I mean?**
Rachel:	Yes, I do. It *is* stressful.
Kate:	That's why I'm thinking about living at home next year.
Rachel:	**What are you saying?** We agreed to get a flat together.
Kate:	I know, but I'm not sure. **What I mean is** I'd prefer to live with my family and concentrate on my studies.

Conversation 4

Frank:	Look at how much revision I have to do for the exams next week! It's impossible.
Paula:	It's not impossible. You need to plan your week. That's all.
Frank:	**What do you mean?**
Paula:	**Don't get me wrong,** there is a lot of revision, but you just need to make a study diary and have a goals chart.
Frank:	**Sorry, I don't get you.**
Paula:	Look at mine. This is a study diary. So tomorrow is Tuesday – I'm going to revise Geography and English. It's like you make an appointment.
Frank:	Oh, **I see.** Great idea!

2 Add the bold phrases from the conversations to complete the boxes below.

Repeating something in different words	Asking someone to explain their view
1 Don't get me wrong,	9 What do you mean?
2	10 ....
3	11 ....
4	
Checking someone understands	**Saying if I understand or not**
5 See what I mean?	12 ....
6	13 ....
7	14 ....
8	

Saying it accurately

1 The first word of each sentence is missing. Add the correct word. Use the phrases in Conversations, exercise 2 to help you.

1 .... get me wrong, we do have lots of work, but we can do it!

2 .... I'm trying to say is that the journey is pretty long.

3 .... I mean is, I don't enjoy travelling.

4 .... what I mean?

5 .... that make sense?

6 ...., I don't get you.

2 Choose one of the following purposes for each sentence and question in exercise 1:

- explaining something again
- checking someone understands me
- saying I don't understand.

Saying it clearly

62

1 Read and listen to the phrases and questions below. Pay attention to the linked sounds and how the two words join together.

1 What I'm trying to say_is...

2 What I mean_is...

3 See what_I mean?

4 Know what_I mean?

5 What do_you mean?

6 Got_it!

(2) Listen and repeat.

Saying it appropriately

(1) Read and listen to the questions below. Pay attention to the underlined stressed words in each question.

63

1 See what I <u>mean</u>?   **2** Is that <u>right</u>?   **3** <u>What</u> do you <u>mean</u>?

(2) Listen and repeat.

(3) Say the questions below out loud. Underline the stressed word in each sentence.

1 Know what I mean?   **2** Does that make sense?   **3** What are you saying?

(4) Listen and check. Then listen again and repeat. Remember to use rising intonation on the final word of the question.

64

Useful tip: rising intonation in questions

When checking for understanding, rising intonation is a common spoken feature with teenagers in many English-speaking countries. Listen carefully to these speakers in films and programmes.

Get speaking

(1) Read the situations below and think about useful phrases and questions you can use in the conversations. Then play the audio and give your responses.

65

1 Today is your first day in a new job. Your colleague is explaining how to do something.
- Ask one question to check you understand your colleague.
- Then say you understand.

2 Your friend asks for your advice about how to plan her studying.
- Explain how you plan your study (for example, a study diary and a goals chart).
- Then explain how you plan your study again and check your friend understands.

(2) Close your book and listen to the audio again. Try to give your responses without using your notes.

My review

I can explain something again and check someone understands.	❏
I can use phrases to show I do or do not understand.	❏
I can ask someone to explain something to me.	❏
I can use correct word stress and rising intonation.	❏

12 LISTENING TO PROBLEMS

Getting started

1 Who do you talk to when you have problems? Do you feel better after talking to him/her?

2 When did you last listen to a friend's problems? Did you help him/her?

Conversations

66

Read and listen to the three conversations. Which one involves a problem:

a at work ....

b at home ....

c at college ....

Conversation 1

Rob: What's up? Are you OK?

Bella: No, not really. It's my job. I'm not enjoying it and I didn't get the promotion.

Rob: Oh dear. **Why don't you** talk to your boss and ask for his advice?

Bella: I tried. He's not very helpful. He said he was busy and didn't have time to talk.

Rob: Well, **you need to** try again. **You should** tell him it's important.

Bella: I don't see the point. He gave the promotion to Sam, my colleague.

Rob: Oh. **If I were you, I'd** look for another job. Why don't we look online at vacancies and get some ideas?

Bella: Yeah. **That sounds great. Thanks for listening to me.**

Language note

If I were you, I'd... has a similar meaning to *You could...* It is used to give advice to someone and make suggestions.

***If I were you, I'd** look for another job.*

***You could** look for a different job.*

Conversation 2

Professor: Your essay was late again. You need to submit the essays on time, Ben.

Shane: I know. I'm sorry, Professor. I don't know what to do. I'm struggling this year. There's never enough time. I have loads of lectures, I spend hours in the library studying and researching, I'm involved in lots of clubs, I have football training three times a week ...

Professor: OK, OK. Calm down. **We need to** help you plan and organise your time. **You should** book a place on the next time management course. I think the courses run every month in the library.

Shane: Thanks, Professor. **That sounds like a great idea! I really appreciate your help.**

Conversation 3

Mum: Are you sure you've got everything?

Julie: Everything's fine, Mum. I've packed all my things. Everything is sorted and I'm ready for college!

Mum: When you get there, **you should** unpack and then go to the welcome party. It's difficult making new friends, but—

Julie: Don't worry, Mum. **Why don't you** visit Aunt Sue this afternoon? It'll take your mind off things. I'll text you when I get there and call you tonight.

Mum: Yes. **That's a good plan.**

2 Read and listen to the conversations again. For each conversation, what is the problem and what is the suggestion?

problem	suggestion

3 Complete the table below with the bold phrases from the conversations.

suggestions	responses
Why don't you ... ?	

Saying it accurately

1 Complete the gaps in the suggestions with a word from the box below.

don't	need	should	were

1 You .... speak to your teacher about it.

2 I think you .... to make a schedule for your studying.

3 If I .... you, I'd buy a new laptop.

4 Why .... you meet your friends and relax?

2 Put the words in the correct order to make sentences.

1 really appreciate I help your ....

2 situation It's a complicated ....

3 like sounds That a idea great ....

4 to know do I don't what ....

5 confused I really feel ....

6 to Thanks listening me for ....

7 I'm course my struggling with ....

3 Which sentences in exercise 2 are responses to a suggestion?

Saying it clearly

1 Read the sentences below and underline the contractions. Which sentence has a negative contraction?

1 It's difficult.

2 I'm struggling.

3 I'd buy a newspaper.

4 That's not fair.

5 What's up?

6 Why don't you call her?

2 Listen to the sentences. Pay attention to the contractions.
67

3 Listen again and repeat.

Saying it appropriately

1 Read the sentences below. What is the speaker's reason for saying these sentences? Look back at the conversations to help you.

1 Oh dear.

2 OK, OK. Calm down

3 Everything's fine.

4 Don't worry.

Useful tip: sympathetic intonation

It is important to use sympathetic intonation to show your feelings. For example, when you are listening to someone with a problem, speak gently, and in a low tone.

Oh dear. That's not fair.

---

2 Listen and repeat the sentences. Try to copy how the speaker says the sentences.
68

Get speaking

1 Read the following problems and make notes to prepare what you are going to say. Use your imagination or the phrases from Conversations, exercise 3 to help you. Then play the audio and give your responses.
69

1 Your sister doesn't like her teacher and isn't enjoying her course at college.

- say something to make her feel better
- suggest something to help with the problem

2 Your mother is worried about you going on a school trip.

- say something to make her feel better
- suggest something to help with the problem

2 Close your book and listen to the audio again. Try to give your responses without using your notes.

My review

I can talk about problems and make suggestions. ☐

I can give responses to the suggestions. ☐

I can say contractions accurately. ☐

I can use helpful and sympathetic intonation. ☐

13 MAKING A COMPLAINT

Getting started

1 Have you ever made a complaint in English? What was it about?

2 How do you think the woman in the picture is feeling?

Conversations

70

Read and listen to the three conversations. What are the people complaining about?

a food ....   b a flight ....   c a mobile phone..........

Conversation 1

Eddie: Hello, I bought this cell phone last month, but **there seems to be a problem** with the screen. Look, it doesn't work.

Assistant: **Oh dear.** You're right. **I'm very sorry about that. Can I offer you a** full refund or an exchange?

Eddie: **I'd like** an exchange, please.

Assistant: No problem. Do you have the receipt?

Eddie: No, I don't. I lost it.

Assistant: I'm afraid I can't help you without the receipt ...

Eddie: Well, **that's not good enough.** The phone was very expensive and now I can't use it.

Assistant: I understand that, but we do need the receipt, I'm afraid. Perhaps you can get it repaired? There's a repair shop at the end of the street.

Useful tip: polite and strong complaints

You can make your complaint polite or very strong.

Verbs like *seem* and *appear* make the complaint more polite.

There seems to be a problem with the screen. (= I'm not sure what the problem is.)

Specific phrases make the complaint very strong.

That's not good enough. (= This situation is not what I want.)

Conversation 2

Angela:	Good morning, customer service. Angela speaking, How can I help you?
Jim:	Good morning, **I'm phoning to complain about** the flight I was on yesterday.
Angela:	**Oh, I'm sorry to hear that.** Can you explain the problem to me?
Jim:	Well, **the first problem was that** there was a delay at the airport. Then we boarded the plane and the screen in front of my seat didn't work. The stewards were really unhelpful too. Then finally, when the flight landed, we waited for our luggage but it didn't arrive.
Angela:	Oh, I'm sorry to hear that. Our aim is to give excellent customer service to all our passengers and **I'm so sorry we let you down.**
Jim:	Well, yes, I'm very annoyed.
Angela:	If you give me your details, I'll investigate your lost luggage.
Jim:	Oh, thank you. That's great.I appreciate your help.

Conversation 3

Waitress:	Here you are. The chicken for you, sir. And the fish for you, madam.
Sally:	**Sorry, but** I didn't order the fish. I ordered the steak.
Waitress:	Oh, did you? I'll change that for you.
Harry:	Actually, I don't think this chicken is cooked.
Waitress:	I'm very sorry. I'm afraid we're very busy today. But I'll tell the chef and he'll prepare fresh meals for you.
Harry:	**I don't want to make a fuss but** we waited 45 minutes for these meals. I'm really disappointed with your service. I'd like to speak to the manager.
Waitress:	He's not here today. But I could—
Harry:	No, thank you. We're leaving. Come on, Sally. Let's go.

Useful tip: using 'I'm afraid...'

I'm afraid... means *I'm sorry to tell you that...* . Use it to make an apology. You can put it at the beginning or end of a sentence.

***I'm afraid** we're very busy today.*

*We're very busy today, **I'm afraid**.*

2   Read and listen to the conversations again. Are these statements true or false? Put a tick (✓) in the correct column.

		True	False
1	Eddie would like a refund.	....	....
2	The assistant suggests getting the mobile repaired.	....	....
3	Angela offers to investigate Jim's lost luggage.	....	....
4	Jim is pleased at the end of the conversation.	....	....
5	Sally ordered the fish.	....	....
6	Harry and Sally waited an hour.	....	....
7	The manager speaks to Harry.	....	....

3   Put the bold phrases in the conversations into the correct category below.

Making a complaint	Responding to a complaint
1	1 ....
2	2 ....
3	3 ....
4	4 ....
5	5 ....
6	

Saying it accurately

1   Match the beginnings (1–7) and endings (a–g) to make complete sentences.

1	That's not	a	to be a problem.
2	I'm very sorry	b	to complain about...
3	There seems	c	about that.
4	I don't want	d	let you down.
5	I'm phoning	e	good enough.
6	The first	f	problem was that
7	I'm so sorry we	g	to make a fuss but...

2   Which sentence in exercise 1 is the strongest way to make a complaint? Which phrase do you think is the most polite way to respond to a complaint?

Saying it clearly

71

1   Read and listen to the sentences below. Are the underlined words stressed (strong) or unstressed (weak)? Which sound is in each of these words?

1   There seems <u>to</u> be <u>a</u> problem.

2   I don't want <u>to</u> make <u>a</u> fuss but <u>the</u> food isn't cooked.

3   I'm phoning <u>to</u> complain about <u>the</u> flight.

Useful tip: sentence stress and using the schwa sound

Practise sentence stress and using the schwa sound when you speak, because it helps you sound like a natural English speaker. Some common unstressed words are *a*, *the*, *to*.

2 Listen again and repeat. Practise using the weak stress and the schwa sound.

Saying it appropriately

1 Listen to two different speakers reading the sentences below. For sentences 1–3, decide which speaker (a or b) sounds more confident. For sentences 4 and 5, decide which speaker sounds more honest.

1 That's not good enough.

2 The first problem was that the parcel didn't arrive.

3 I'm phoning to complain about the laptop I bought.

4 I'm very sorry about that.

5 I'm so sorry we let you down.

2 Listen to the sentences again. This time you're going to hear the confident speakers for sentences 1–3 and the honest speakers in 4 and 5. Listen and repeat.

Get speaking

1 Read the situations below. Prepare what you're going to say and make notes. Refer to the phrases in Conversations, exercise 3 and the intonation practice in Saying it appropriately exercise 2 to help you. Then listen to the audio and make your complaints.

1 You bought a new mobile last week. It stopped working yesterday.

- return to the shop and make a complaint
- say you want an exchange
- say you have the receipt

2 You go to an expensive restaurant with your friend for lunch. The waitress brings the wrong order for your friend.

- tell the waitress what your friend ordered
- say your food doesn't look cooked
- say you are really disappointed then leave the restaurant

My review

I can make a complaint in different situations.	❏
I can use suitable verbs (*seem* or *appear*) to sound polite.	❏
I can use schwa sounds and weak stress correctly.	❏
I can sound confident when making a complaint.	❏
I can sound sincere when responding to a complaint.	❏

14 MAKING AN APOLOGY

Getting started

1 When did you last make an apology?

2 How did you feel? How did the other person feel?

3 What words or phrases do you use to make an apology?

Conversations

75

Read and listen to the four conversations. Which conversations include someone who forgives (= stops feeling angry at) the person making the apology?

Conversation 1 ☐   Conversation 3 ☐

Conversation 2 ☐   Conversation 4 ☐

Conversation 1

Pete: **I'm sorry to disturb you**, Chris. Do you have a minute?

Chris: What's the problem?

Pete: **I wanted to apologise for** getting the figures wrong in this morning's presentation. I was very embarrassed about the mess up. **I'm terribly sorry.**

Chris: Oh, thanks, Pete. I appreciate that. **Don't worry.** We all make mistakes. We're all human!

Pete: Yeah, I suppose so! Thank you, Chris.

Conversation 2

Neil: Hi Diane. **Sorry I'm late.** The traffic was terrible, and there was nowhere to park.

Diane: I got here at 7. That's nearly an hour ago! We've missed the start of the film now.

Neil: OK. I said I'm sorry. I don't want to **fall out over it**. It's not a big deal, is it?

Diane: It is to me. You're always late. I really wanted to see the film.

Neil: I'll buy you a pizza to **make up for it**. Come on.

Diane: OK. **Let's forget about it.**

Conversation 3

Debs: Hello, what's wrong?

Louise: What's wrong? You missed my party last week, and **you didn't even say sorry.**

Debs: I sent you a text. **I'm really sorry.** I was just too tired.

Louise: I was really upset that you didn't come.

Debs: Oh no. **I didn't want to upset you. I'm so sorry.**

Louise: You did upset me. You really hurt my feelings.

Conversation 4

Vicky: **I wanted to say sorry** about last night. I was tired and a bit grumpy.

James: You were very rude to me.

Vicky: I know, and. **I really regret it.** I'm sorry.

James: Do you remember what you said?

Vicky: **I didn't mean it.** Can I **make it up to** you? Cook you dinner?

James: **Apology accepted.** And yes, you can cook me dinner!

2 Complete the summary of each conversation with a name.

1 .... apologises for getting figures wrong.

2 .... had problems driving to meet his friend.

3 .... made her friend sad but didn't realise.

4 .... doesn't want to argue and forgives his friend.

3 Look at the conversations again. Which three adverbs are used before *sorry*? How do the adverbs change the apology?

4 Add the bold phrases from the conversation to complete the boxes below.

introduce an apology	mean 'I forgive you'
1 I wanted to apologise for	8 Apology accepted.
2	9 ....
offer to do something as part of the apology	**ask for permission to talk to someone**
3 make up for it	10 ....
4	
explain the apology	**apologise for not arriving on time**
5 I didn't want to upset you.	11 ....
6	
7	

Saying it accurately

1 Put the words in the correct order to make sentences. Which sentence would you probably not use with friends?

1 to sorry I'm disturb you

2 want I you to didn't upset

3 forget Let's about it

4 sorry I'm I'm late

5 didn't I it mean

2 Complete the sentences with the missing prepositions. Read and listen to the conversation again to help you.

1 I wanted to apologise .... my mistake yesterday.

2 Can I make it up .... you?

3 I don't want to fall out .... it.

4 Let's forget .... it.

5 I'll buy you a present to make .... for it.

3 Complete the missing letters in the phrases. Then match the phrases to the correct definition.

1 Let's not f.......... o.......... over it. It doesn't matter.

2 You have to m.......... u.......... f.......... arriving an hour late.

3 I'm going to m.......... i.......... u.......... t......... you.

a do something nice to change a bad situation

b argue and stop being friends

c do something nice for somebody to change a bad situation

Saying it clearly

1 Underline all the contractions in the sentences below.

1 I didn't mean it.

2 I didn't want to upset you.

3 Don't worry.

4 You didn't even say sorry.

5 I'm sorry I'm late.

2 How many syllables are in each contraction?

1 .... 2 .... 3 .... 4 .... 5 ....

3 Listen and repeat.

76

Useful tip: saying contractions clearly

It is important to use accurate pronunciation when using contractions in a sentence. Then the person who is listening will clearly understand what you are saying.

Saying it appropriately

77

1 Listen to two speakers saying the sentences below. Which speaker (a or b) is making a real apology?

1 I wanted to say sorry.

2 I'm terribly sorry.

3 I regret it.

4 I didn't mean it.

5 I'm sorry to disturb you.

6 I'm sorry I'm late.

78

2 Now listen to the speakers making the real apologies. Listen again and repeat.

Get speaking

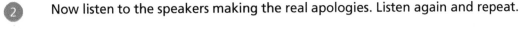
79

1 Read the following situations and make notes to prepare what you are going to say. Then play the audio and give your answers.

1 You had a long day at work yesterday and felt very tired. You were angry with your flatmate and shouted at him.

- make your apology

- explain your apology and offer to do something

2 You are waiting for your friend but he is very late.

- tell him how you feel

- accept the apology

3 You want to talk to a colleague but she is very busy.

- ask if you can interrupt

- apologize for missing a meeting and explain why

2 Close your book and listen to the audio again. Try to give your responses without using your notes.

My review

I can apologise in formal and informal situations.	☐
I can use adverbs to make my apology stronger.	☐
I can use the correct prepositions in apologies.	☐
I can use contractions and syllables correctly.	☐
I can make apologies that sound real.	☐

---

15 SHOWING SYMPATHY

Getting started

1 What happened to the man in the photo?
2 How do you think he is feeling?
3 What would you say to show sympathy (= make someone feel better)?

Conversations

80

Read and listen to the four conversations. Match the conversation with the topic below.

a car accident ....
b job search ....
c learning to drive ....
d sports injury ....

Conversation 1

Paul: Thanks for visiting me, Nick. It's very kind of you.

Nick: That's what friends are for. How are you feeling?

Paul: Not great. My leg's very painful.

Nick: How did it happen? Can you remember?

Paul: **It's my own fault.** I was skiing too fast and I lost control. I couldn't stop. Then the rescue team took a long time to find me. It was really scary, to be honest.

Nick: **I can imagine.** Well, never mind. You're safe now.

Paul: Yes, the doctor said it's amazing that I only broke my leg. So I'm very lucky.

Conversation 2

Phil: What's wrong?

Emma: I failed my driving test. I can't believe it.

Phil: **Oh, I'm sorry.** What happened?

Emma: I made some mistakes. I was really nervous.

Phil: **Oh dear.** I think everybody feels nervous before taking their test. I was terrified.

Emma: I feel so stupid. All my friends have a driving licence.

Phil:	Cheer up. It's not the end of the world.
Emma:	I suppose so. I can take the test again soon.
Phil:	See? It's not that bad.

Useful tip: useful expressions

Learn useful expressions for different situations. When you want to make someone feel better about something, you can use the following expressions.

Never mind.
Don't worry about it.
Try not to worry.

Conversation 3

Alan:	Hi, Sarah. Listen, I can't make the presentation today. I had a car accident last night.
Sarah:	**That's awful!** Are you OK? Where are you?
Alan:	I'm at home now. I got a taxi downtown last night and another car hit us.
Sarah:	**How frightening!** Are you hurt?
Alan:	I'm OK, thanks. The ambulance took the taxi driver to hospital. I think he's OK.
Sarah:	**That's good news. Why don't you try to** relax now and get some sleep? I'll take care of the presentation.
Alan:	Yeah, I will. Thanks, Sarah.
Sarah:	**Call me if you need anything.**

Conversation 4

Carl:	Hello?
James:	Hi, Carl. It's James Henson from the recruitment agency.
Carl:	Hi, James. Any news on the job yet? Did I get it?
James:	No, I'm afraid they offered the job to someone else.
Carl:	Oh, no! That job was perfect for me.
James:	**I know how you feel,** but it was a good interview. **Try not to worry.** It was your first job application since you graduated, so there's lots of time to find the right job. **Stay positive.**

2 Answer the questions below.

1 Which phrase shows Paul thinks he is responsible for the accident?

2 Which phrase shows Nick understands how Paul felt?

3 Which phrases does Phil use to show sympathy to Emma?

4 Which phrases does Phil use to help Emma feel better?

5 Which phrases show Sarah's reaction to Alan's news?

6 Which phrases does Sarah use to help Alan feel better?

7 Which phrase does James use to say he understands?

8 Which phrases does James use to give encouragement to Carl?

Useful tip: talking about pain

Learn the different forms and uses of new words. For example, *pain* often appears in particular phrases.

*I've got **a pain** in my leg.*   *It is **painful**.*   *I'm **in pain**.*

Saying it accurately

1 Complete the conversations with the words from the box. There are two extra words.

awful	mind	own	sorry	worry

1 I had an accident on my scooter this morning.

That's .... ! How are you feeling now?

2 How did it happen? Do you remember anything?

It's my .... fault. I knew the mountains were dangerous and I was going too fast.

3 I failed one of my exams. I have to take it again next semester.

Oh, I'm .... to hear that. That's bad news.

81

2 Listen and check.

3 Complete the phrases with verbs. Use your answers to Conversations, exercise 2 to help you.

1 I .... imagine. It sounds frightening.

2 It .... the end of the world.

3 Why .... you try to relax?

4 Call me if you .... anything.

5 I .... how you feel.

6 Try not to ....

Saying it appropriately

Language note

When you are helping a friend, remember the following rules:

1   speak at a slower pace to show you are listening to the problem

2   speak in a lower tone to show the conversation is personal

If you don't use these techniques, you may sound unkind or uncaring.

1   Read the sentences below. Think about the two techniques in the language note and imagine saying the sentences.

Oh, I'm sorry. ....
That's awful! ....
It's not that bad. ....
I know how you feel. ....
Cheer up. It's not the end of the world. ....
Call me if you need anything. ....
Try not to worry. ....

82   **2**   Listen to the sentences. Do the speakers use the techniques in the language note? Put a tick (✓) if the speaker uses the two techniques in the language note above. Put a cross (✗) if not.

Get speaking

83   **1**   Read the following situations and make notes to prepare what you are going to say. Then play the audio and give your answers.

1   Your friend is in hospital after an accident.
   * show your sympathy
   * tell him you understand how he feels
2   Your friend has failed a test at school.
   * show your sympathy
   * then give some encouragement
3   You tell a colleague that she didn't get a new job in your department.
   * show you understand
   * give some encouragement

My review

I can understand someone talking about their problems.	❑
I can react to someone's bad news and make them feel better.	❑
I can correctly pronounce unstressed (weak) words and the schwa sound.	❑
I can use suitable intonation when helping a friend.	❑

16 SAYING 'THANK YOU'

Getting started

1 What different ways can you say 'thank you' in actions and words?
2 Think about the last time you either said 'thank you' or showed your thanks to someone. What did he/she do to help you?

Conversations

Read and listen to the seven conversations. Where do you think the conversations are happening? How do the speakers in each conversation know each other?

Conversation 1

Hi, Aunt Sue. I'm just phoning to say thank you for coming to my party. I hope you enjoyed it. **Thank you so much** for the present. I love the watch. Give me a call when you get this message. Bye.

Conversation 2

A: We're going to a picnic on Saturday. Do you want to come?
B: **I'd love to but** I'm busy. I'm visiting my sister this weekend.
A: Oh, that's a shame. Maybe another time?
B: Yeah. **Thanks for asking.**

> **Useful tip:** not accepting an invitation
>
> It is polite to explain why you are unable to accept an invitation or offer.
>
> *I'd love to but I'm busy, I'm visiting my sister this weekend.*

Conversation 3

A: Here's your coffee and your change.
B: Cheers.
A: No problem.

Conversation 4

A: **Thanks for** dinner. It was delicious.

B: **I'm glad you liked it.**

A: Next time, come to my apartment and I can cook for you.

Conversation 5

A: Excuse me, can you give me a hand with these boxes?

B: Sorry, I'm afraid I've got a problem with my back and I can't carry anything heavy.

C: **Let me help you.** I'll take this box.

B: Thanks, **I appreciate it.** It's really heavy.

C: **You're welcome.**

Conversation 6

A: Need a lift home?

B: Yes, please. **Thanks for asking.** I'm too tired to walk home.

A: **No worries.** Let's go.

Conversation 7

A: Here's your drink. I ordered some sandwiches for us too.

B: **Thanks.** I'm starving.

A: **That's OK.**

2 Read and listen to the conversations again. In which conversations do people refuse or say no to something? What reason do the people give?

3 Put the bold phrases from the conversations in the correct category.

saying thanks to a friend	saying 'no thanks'
1	1 ....
2	
3	

saying thanks in a more formal situation	responding to others saying thanks
1	1 ....
2	2 ....
	3 ....
	4 ....
	5 ....

Useful tip: 'to thank' (verb)

Use the verb *to thank* for more formal situations and speeches such as weddings or awards.

*I'd like **to thank** my family for supporting me.*

Saying it accurately

1 Read the situations below and circle the two best responses.

1 Your friend passes you a pen.

   a Cheers.   **b** Thanks.   **c** Thank you very much.

2 Your colleague helps you with a difficult project.

   a Cheers.   **b** Thank you so much.   **c** Thanks for helping me.

3 Your grandparents buy you a very expensive gift for your graduation.

   a Cheers.   **c** Thank you very much.

   b Thank you so much for the present.

2 Complete the responses with the missing words.

1 .... love to but I'm busy.   **4** .... worries.

2 .... problem.   **5** .... OK.

3 .... glad you liked it.

Saying it clearly

85 **1** Listen to the words below and pay attention to the underlined sounds.

1 <u>Ch</u>eers!   **3** I do appre<u>ci</u>ate it.

2 <u>Th</u>ank you.   **4** My plea<u>s</u>ure.

86 **2** Listen to the sounds 1 to 4. Then match the sounds to the words (a–d).

a <u>Th</u>ank you. 2   **c** <u>Ch</u>eers! ....

b My plea<u>s</u>ure. ....   **d** I do appre<u>ci</u>ate it. ....

87 **3** Listen and check. Then listen again and repeat.

Saying it appropriately

1 Read the phrases below. Underline the words which you think will describe all of the speakers.

angry   bored   friendly   genuine   polite

1 Cheers.

2 Thanks for asking.

3 Thank you so much.

4 I'd love to but I'm away.

5 No problem.

6 I'm glad you liked it.

7 You're welcome.

8 That's OK.

2 Listen and check your ideas.
88

3 Listen again and repeat.

Get speaking

1 Read the situations below and think about how you're going to express your thanks.

1 Your colleague helps you prepare notes for an important presentation.

2 Your parents buy you a very expensive gift for your graduation.

3 Your friend invites you to a party on Saturday. You are busy at the weekend.

2 Listen to the other speaker. Express your thanks when you hear the beep.
89

3 Read the situations below and think about how you're going to respond to the other speaker saying thanks.

1 You buy your friend a drink.

2 You give your friend a lift home.

3 You cook your friend a delicious lunch.

4 Listen to the other speaker. Express your thanks when you hear the beep.
90

My review

I can say 'no thank you' politely.	❏
I can express thanks to a friend and in more formal situations.	❏
I can respond to someone thanking me.	❏
I can use correct sounds and intonation when expressing thanks.	❏

17 AGREEING AND DISAGREEING

Getting started

1 Where are the two people?
2 What are they talking about?
3 What do you think they are saying?

Conversations

91

Read and listen to Sarah and Tony and then Clare and Andrew. Then answer the questions opposite. Listen again if necessary.

Conversation 1

Sarah: So, what did you think?

Tony: **Actually**, I really enjoyed it.

Sarah: Me too. And did you like Steve Green?

Tony: Well, **to be honest**, I'm not a big fan of his.

Sarah: Really? He's won two Oscars.

Tony: **I'm just saying**, I don't think he's a very good actor.

Sarah: But you liked the film?

Tony: Yeah, I did. I just don't like him. **It's no big deal.**

Conversation 2

Clare: Did you go to that talk? **You know**, the one about summer jobs in France.

Andrew: **Actually**, yes. I applied yesterday and I've got an interview next week! **Isn't that great?**

Clare: **I suppose so, but** shouldn't you think about it first? **What I mean is**, there are lots of things to find out: application forms, visas, accommodation, qualifications and training.

Andrew: **Maybe, but** the university organises everything. It's pretty easy.

Clare: But what about living in another country? Or speaking another language? Are you worried about that? I would be really nervous.

Andrew: **I know what you mean, but** they have a residential course in the first week, so we can make friends and improve our French.

Conversation 1

1 Do Sarah and Tony have a formal or an informal relationship?

2 What is Tony's opinion about the actor?

Conversation 2

3 Do you think Andrew and Clare are about the same age or different ages?

4 What does Clare think about Andrew's plans?

Useful tip: using 'well...'

Use *well...* to introduce an opinion someone may not like. It is more polite.

Well, to be honest, I don't think he's a very good actor.
Well, I didn't like the film. I thought it was boring.

---

2 Look at the bold words and phrases in Conversation 1. Add them to the table below.

	Conversation 1	Conversation 2
introduce a positive opinion	1	
introduce a negative opinion	2	
explain your opinion 'isn't very important'	3	
	4	
agree but then disagree	5	6
		7
		8
repeat and expand your opinion		9
		10

3 Look at the bold words and phrases in Conversation 2. Add them to the table in exercise 2.

Useful tip: expressing you opinion

How you express your opinion is very important.

• Firstly, you have to choose the correct words and phrases to not upset and offend other people.

• Secondly, you have to use the correct intonation when you speak, so you don't sound rude or angry.

Saying it accurately

1 Look at the dialogue and add a–c below to the correct place.

1 So do you like the exhibition? ....

2 Good! This is my favourite painting. It's beautiful. ....

3 Why not? He's your favourite artist. What's wrong with it?....................

a To be honest, I don't like it.

b I'm just saying, I don't like it.

c Actually, I really like it.

2 Complete the dialogue with the phrases below.

I know what you mean	but to be honest	You know

Don: Did you go to that new cafe last week? **1** ....….. the one by the river?

Fiona: Yes, it's really nice. The only problem is the traffic is bad and there's nowhere to park.

Don: **2** ...….. you could get a bus. It's near the bus station.

Fiona: That's true, but I prefer driving. **3** ...….. , I think the buses are dirty and really noisy.

Saying it clearly

92

1 Listen to the phrases below. Pay attention to the words that link together. Can you hear the bold letters?

1 I'm jus**t**_saying

2 Wh**a**t_I mean_is

3 I **k**now_ **wh**at_you_mean, but

4 I suppose_**s**o, but

2 Listen again and repeat the phrases.

Useful tip: linking words and sounds

Linking words and sounds together helps you to 'connect' your speech and sound natural.

What_I mean_is, there are lots of things to find out.
I suppose_so, but I still don't like it.

Saying it appropriately

1 Read the sentences. Which do you think will sound positive, negative or neutral (not positive or negative)?

	Positive	Negative	Neutral
1 Actually, I really enjoyed it.	....	....	....
2 Do you see what I'm saying?	....	....	....
3 I'm just saying, I didn't like it.	....	....	....
4 I'm not keen on it. It's no big deal.	....	....	....
5 To be honest, I don't like that song.	....	....	....
6 Well, as you know, I visited the city last week.	....	....	....
7 What I mean is, you have to think about it.	....	....	....

2 Listen and check your answers.

3 Listen again and repeat.

Get speaking

1 You're going to have two conversations about (1) an album and (2) an essay. Listen to the speakers and give your opinion after the beep. Use instructions 1–5 to help you.

Conversation 1

1 Introduce a positive opinion. Say you really liked the album.

2 Introduce a negative opinion. Say you don't like that track.

3 Explain your opinion isn't very important. Say you don't like it.

Conversation 2

4 Repeat and expand your opinion. Tell the speaker he has to write in a formal tone.

5 Agree but then disagree. Explain he studied formal and informal letters last semester.

2 Listen to the speakers again and give your opinion. Try to answer without looking at your book.

My review

I can introduce a positive opinion and a negative opinion. ❏

I can agree and give a different opinion. ❏

I can agree but then disagree. ❏

I can give opinions accurately and appropriately. ❏

18 STRONGER OPINIONS

Getting started

1 Describe what is happening in the photo.
2 What do you say when you strongly disagree with someone?
3 How easy is it to agree and disagree when you are speaking English?

Conversations

95

Read and listen to the four conversations.

a For each conversation, do the people have the same opinion or a different opinion?

1 .... 2 .... 3 .... 4 ....

b Which person shows very strong disagreement? ....

Conversation 1

Mark: Did you read that article about university tuition fees?

Henry: Yes, it's terrible. I think students should pay their own tuition fees, not the government.

Mark: **How can you say that?** The government needs to look after the next generation and help them. They are the future. In my opinion—

Henry: **Sorry to butt in, but** there are lots of students who waste time and money at university. They don't help our country, so why give them money? A student should study and work part-time.

Mark: **Really? Do you think so?**

Henry: Yes, absolutely. It teaches them responsibility.

Mark: Well, I suppose **I can see your point.**

Conversation 2

Gina: Do you want some lunch? My mom cooked my favourite dishes for me. And she's going to come and visit next weekend and help me with the assignment we have to do.

Tony: Are you serious? Your mom is going to help you with the assignment!

Gina: I don't understand the module, to be honest. I need a good grade, so mom's my only option.

Tony: **That's ridiculous!** It's cheating. We're at college and we're here to learn.

Gina: I don't see the problem. **I guess you have your opinion and I have mine.**

Conversation 3

Sharon: Mike, remember I won't be at work next week – I'm on holiday. I'm flying to New Zealand. I can't wait!

Mike: Mmm. We're having a 'holiday at home' this summer. It's important to be green. Think about the air pollution and the fuel a plane needs. It's really bad for the environment.

Sharon: **Can I just say that** pollution isn't only from flying? You drive your car everywhere. We live in a small town, so you could walk, cycle, take the bus ...

Mike: Yeah, OK, **I get your point. But** I do work unsocial hours so I need my car to get to work. Anyway, **I think we're both basically saying the same thing** – we both care about the environment.

Useful tip: showing you understand

It is polite to listen to other people's opinions. Try to show you understand their viewpoint on the topic.

Yeah, OK, I get your point. But I think getting the bus is a good idea.

Conversation 4

Fran: Morning, Rosa. You look tired. Did you work late again last night? I think we need to have a chat later on.

Rosa: **Excuse me?**

Fran: **What I'm trying to say is** you're working too hard. We need to discuss how we can reduce your hours—

Rosa: **Let me stop you there.** We are working really hard, because we've just started a new business, but my job is fun.

Fran: I know, but none of us should be working seven days a week.

Rosa: Running your own business is hard work, but I'm enjoying it, honestly. **What I will say is** you could always join me ...

Language note

It's important to learn and use complete phrases (a set of words). The meaning for the phrase is different to the meaning of individual words in the phrase.

No, let me stop you there. = Stop speaking, because I want to speak.

Can I say something? = I'd like to speak.

2 Complete the categories with the bold phrases from the conversations.

Commenting on an opinion

1 ....

2 ....

3 ....

4 ....

5 ....

6 ....

Giving your opinion

1 ....

2 ....

3 ....

4 ....

5 ....

6 ....

Concluding an agreement and disagreement

1 ....

2 ....

3 ....

Saying it accurately

1 Match the beginnings (1–6) and ends (a–f) of the phrases.

1	How can you	**a**	to say is...
2	Really? Do you	**b**	opinion and I have mine.
3	What I'm trying	**c**	think so?
4	OK, I get	**d**	saying the same thing.
5	You have your	**e**	your point but...
6	I think we're both	**f**	say that?

2 Listen and check. Then listen again and repeat.
96

Saying it clearly

1 Read and listen to the sentences below. Pay attention to the stressed (strong) underlined words.
97

1 That's <u>ridiculous</u>!

2 Are you <u>serious</u>?

Useful tip: giving strong opinions

Stress the important words in the sentence when you are disagreeing or giving your opinion. This shows how strong and confident your opinion is.

<u>Excuse</u> me?

(2) Read the phrases below. Which words do you think are stressed (strong)? Practise saying the sentences out loud.

1 Can I just say that...

2 What I will say is...

(3) Listen and check. Then listen again and repeat.

98

Saying it appropriately

(1) Read the sentences below. Imagine you are strongly disagreeing with someone. Which words are you going to stress? How are you going to say the sentences to show your strong disagreement?

1 Excuse me?

2 No, let me stop you there.

3 What I'm trying to say is...

4 Yes, I get your point but...

5 How can you say that?

(2) Listen and check. Do you sound as strong as the speakers? Listen again and repeat.

99

Get speaking

(1) Read the following situations and make notes to prepare your responses. Then play the audio and give your answers.

100

1 Your friend thinks that driving her car is the best way to travel.

• Comment on her opinion. Suggest that the bus is better.

• Give your opinion.

• Say you understand her opinion, but you both have different opinions

2 Your classmate thinks you study too hard.

• Comment on his opinion.

• Give your opinion. Explain you need good grades and you want to get a scholarship at university.

• Criticise his opinion.

(2) Close your book and listen to the audio again. Try to give your responses without using your notes.

My review

I can comment on another opinion and give my opinion. ❑

I can show I agree and understand another opinion. ❑

I can use correct emphatic stress to express my opinion. ❑

I can use strong and confident intonation to express my opinion. ❑

19 GIVING FEEDBACK

Getting started

1 Think of a time when your friend wanted to buy something, but you didn't like it. What did you say to him/her?

2 Have you received a gift which you didn't like? What did you say to the person who gave you the gift?

Conversations

101

Read and listen to the four conversations. Match each of the descriptions below to a conversation.

a failed exam ....

b horrible clothes ....

c more studying ....

d noisy colleague ....

e office activities ....

f ugly luggage ....

g unwanted gift ....

h wrong size outfit ....

Conversation 1

Louise: Here's the dress I love. What do you think? Does it look OK on me?

Zoe: **Well, I'm not sure.**

Louise: Why? What's wrong with it?

Zoe: **I don't think it suits you. It's a bit** short. Why don't you try this black one?

Louise: But what's wrong with this one?

Zoe: **If I were you, I would** try the black one. I think it, look great.

Language note

We use specific phrases to describe whether something is suitable for someone:

A: *Do you like this orange hat?*

B: *I don't think it suits you.* (= It doesn't look good on you.)

A: *I bought you these jeans. Do you like them?*

B: *They're not really me.* (= They're not my style.)

Conversation 2

Jan:	Sarah, **can I have a quick word?**
Sarah:	Sure, what's wrong?
Jan:	You know this morning, when you were on the phone to head office?
Sarah:	Yes.
Jan:	**I wonder if you could** close your office door when you're on the phone. Then no one will hear your conversation.
Sarah:	It's not private. It's not a problem for me.
Jan:	But **perhaps you should** close the door anyway, so you don't disturb other people. It's not fair on everyone else in the office.

Conversation 3

Mrs Rogers:	**Could we talk about** your speaking test, Kazu?
Kazu:	Yes, did I pass? I was very nervous.
Mrs Rogers:	Sorry Kazu, but I'm afraid you didn't pass. But you gave some good answers. We can look at your answers and find out what areas you need to study.
Kazu:	And then I'll pass the test?
Mrs Rogers:	**I hope so.** You never stop learning a language.

Conversation 4

Tim:	Oh, thanks Uncle Jack. It's very kind of you.
Jack:	My pleasure. I think it's a very smart suitcase. Do you like it?
Tim:	**I'm not sure. It's a bit** old-fashioned.
Jack:	Is it? If you don't like it, we can return it. Then I can buy you something else.
Tim:	Do you mind? **It's not really me, to be honest.**
Jack:	Of course not.

2   Complete the categories below with bold phrases from the conversations.

Expressing an undecided opinion	Giving your opinion	Making a polite request
1 Well, I'm not sure.	1 It's a bit …	1 Can I have a quick word?
2 ………………	2 ………………	2 ………………
	3 ………………	3 ………………
	4 ………………	4 ………………

3 Which category uses modal verbs? Underline the modal verbs.

Saying it accurately

1 Put the words in the correct order to make questions.

1 I Can a have word quick?

2 door I could wonder close if you the?

3 try another you Perhaps should dress?

4 exam Could your about we results talk?

102

2 Listen and check.

3 Complete the conditional sentences with the correct verb below,

close	go	improve	try

1 If I were you, I'd .... another dress.

2 I'd .... the office door, if I were you.

3 If I were you, I'd .... my speaking skills.

4 I'd .... into town this afternoon, if I were you.

Useful tip: giving advice

Use *If I were you, I'd (I would)...* to give advice. The order of the sentence can change – it does not change the meaning.

If I were you, I'd *try the black one.*
I'd try the black one, ***if I were you.***

Saying it clearly

1 Underline the contractions in the sentences below.

1 If I were you, I'd try another one.

2 I'm not sure.

3 I'd buy the black dress, if I were you.

4 It's a bit short.

5 I don't think it suits you.

103

2 Listen and repeat. Pay attention to how the contractions are pronounced.

Saying it appropriately

1 Read the extracts from the conversations. What sounds and pauses do you think are missing in the gaps?

1 .... Well, I'm not sure.

2 .... I don't think it suits you. It's a bit .... short. Why don't you try this black one?

3 .... I'm not sure. It's a bit old-fashioned.

4 .... Do you mind? It's not really .... me, to be honest.

2 Listen and check. Try to complete the gaps.

104

3 Listen again and repeat. Try to use pauses and the natural sounds.

Useful tip: using sounds and pauses

Use speaking techniques like pauses and *er* or *um* sounds to show you are thinking carefully about what you're going to say. The pause is deliberate because it prepares the listener for something upsetting.

Get speaking

1 Read the following situations and make notes to prepare your responses. Then play the audio and give your answers.

105

1 Your friend asks for advice on a coat.
  - Express an unsure opinion to your friend.
  - Give your opinion. Use a conditional sentence.

2 Your classmate is using his mobile and you are trying to study before an exam.
  - Ask if you can talk to him.
  - Make a polite request that he talk somewhere else.
  - Make the request again. Explain why.

2 Close your book and listen to the audio again. Try to give your responses without using your notes.

My review

I can express an undecided opinion.	❏
I can give feedback in formal and informal situations.	❏
I can use conditional sentences to give advice.	❏
I can pronounce contractions correctly.	❏
I can use pauses and natural sounds correctly.	❏

20 SAYING 'WELL DONE!'

Getting started

1 What is happening in the photo?
2 How are they feeling?
3 How do students celebrate this event in your country?

Conversations

106

Read and listen to the four conversations. What are the people celebrating in each conversation? Match each conversation to one of the situations below.

a getting married ....

b getting a job ....

c graduation ....

d getting a car ....

Conversation 1

Craig: Hey, **I wanted to invite you to** my party next month. It's to celebrate my graduation.

Luke: Oh, **well done!** When's the party?

Craig: On the 17th? Are you free?

Luke: Yeah, great.

Craig: Yeah. **It's a big relief.** The final year was difficult and I was worried I'd fail. But I got one of the top marks in my class!

Luke: **That's amazing!**

Conversation 2

Tina: Have you heard? Andy and I are getting married next year!

Celia: **Congratulations! That's wonderful news!**

Tina: Thank you. There are a lot of things to organise. We're choosing a date at the moment. I think it's going to be in September.

Celia: **I'm really pleased for you.** Are you nervous?

Tina: Actually, I'm not nervous at all. **I'm so happy!** I'm over the moon.

Useful tip: showing your interest

It is polite to congratulate someone and then ask how he/she feels. This shows you are interested in his/her good news.

Are you nervous? How are you feeling?

Conversation 3

Fran:	Hey Sam, **guess what?** My dad bought me a car this morning!
Sam:	You're joking!
Fran:	No! **I'm so excited!** It's really nice. It's the one we saw online last week.
Sam:	Wow. **You deserve it.** You studied really hard this year.
Fran:	**Cheers.** So shall I pick you up in my new car this afternoon? We can go to the shopping centre outside town.

Conversation 4

Chris:	Hello?
Russell:	Hey, **I've got something to tell you, dad.** I got the job!
Chris:	What? The sales manager job?
Russell:	Yeah! **I can't believe it.** There were over fifty applicants for the position.
Chris:	Oh, **well done,** Russell! **That's fantastic!**
Russell:	**Thanks.** I'm so pleased. I really wanted that job.
Chris:	**You deserve it.** You work really hard and you prepared a lot for the interview. **I'm proud of you.**
Russell:	Thank you. **That's really kind of you.**

2 Complete the categories below with the bold phrases from the conversations.

Introducing good news	Saying 'well done!'	Responses to 'well done'
1 Guess what?	1 Well done!	1 It's a big relief.
2	2 Congratulations!	2 I can't believe it!
3	3	3 ....
	4	4 ....
	5	5 ....
	6	6 ....
	7	7 ....
	8	

> **Useful tip:** using 'so' for emphasis
>
> Use *so* to emphasise your emotions and how you feel.
>
> *I'm excited.* → *I'm **so** excited.*

Saying it accurately

1 Match a word or phrase with the correct definition below. Use your dictionary to help you.

a	deserve	**1**	collect a person from somewhere
b	over the moon	**2**	be extremely happy
c	pick (somebody) up	**3**	get something because you worked very hard for it
d	proud	**4**	be pleased and satisfied about something/somebody

2 There is one missing word from each sentence. Add the missing word to the correct place.

for	it	of (x2)	tell	to

1 I've got something to .... you.
2 I wanted .... invite you to my party.
3 I'm really pleased .... you.
4 I'm proud .... you.
5 I can't believe .... !
6 That's really kind .... you.

3 Listen and check.

Saying it clearly

1 Read the words below. How many syllables does each word have? Put the words next to the correct stress pattern below.

amazing	congratulations	excited	fantastic
pleased		proud	wonderful

O........................ .... Ooo....................... oOo.......................
.... ooooOo...............................

2 Listen and check. Then listen again and repeat.

Saying it appropriately

1 Read and listen to the sentences below. What punctuation mark do you think is missing from all of these sentences? ......

1 That's amazing
2 That's wonderful news
3 That's fantastic
4 Well done

(2) Listen again and repeat.

Useful tip: sounding excited

Remember to sound excited when you say these exclamations. Imagine saying the sentence with a full stop at the end and think about how this will change the meaning.

---

(3) Listen to two speakers saying the exclamations below. How does each speaker sound? Write E (excited) or J (jealous).

110

	Speaker 1	Speaker 2
1 I'm really pleased for you.		
2 I'm proud of you.		
3 You deserve it.		

(4) Now listen to the excited speaker again and repeat.

111

Get speaking

(1) Read the situations and the instructions below. Think about what you are going to say and make notes if you want.

112

1 Your cousin passed his school exams. He tells you his good news.

   • Say 'well done'.

   • Congratulate him again. Give your opinion on the news (are you pleased? – and/or proud?).

2 You have got a new job and you are very excited.

   • Tell the good news to a friend.

   • Respond to her saying 'well done' to you.

3 Your colleague is getting married. She tells you her good news.

   • Say 'congratulations'.

   • Say 'congratulations' again. Find out how she is feeling.

(2) Listen to the audio again. This time try to give your responses without using your notes.

My review

I can introduce my good news.	❏
I can say 'well done' to someone and respond to 'well done!'.	❏
I can use correct syllable stress on important words.	❏
I can respond to good news with enthusiastic intonation.	❏

MINI-DICTIONARY

Unit 1

ages PLURAL NOUN
a long time • *It's been ages since I last went to the cinema!*

busy ADJECTIVE
full of people who are doing things • *We walked along a busy city street.*

college NOUN
a place where students study after they leave secondary school • *Joan is attending a local college.*

congratulations PLURAL NOUN
used for congratulating someone • *Congratulations on your new job.*

essay NOUN
a short piece of writing on a subject • *We asked Jason to write an essay about his home town.*

internship NOUN
when a student or recent graduate receives practical training in a working environment • *Mark is doing an internship at a publishing company for the summer.*

join VERB
to become a member of an organization • *He joined the Army five years ago.*

journey NOUN
an occasion when you travel from one place to another • *Their journey took them from Paris to Brussels.*

meeting NOUN
an event in which a group of people come together to discuss things or make decisions • *Can we have a meeting to discuss that?*

project NOUN
a plan that takes a lot of time and effort • *The charity is funding a housing project in India.*

take a seat PHRASE
to sit down • *The teacher took a seat in the classroom.*

traffic NOUN
all the vehicles that are on a particular road at one time • *There was heavy traffic on the roads.*

Unit 2

colleague NOUN
a person someone works with • *She's busy talking to a colleague.*

dirty ADJECTIVE
not clean • *She collected the dirty plates from the table.*

expert NOUN
a person who knows a lot about a particular subject • *His brother is a computer expert.*

intelligent ADJECTIVE
able to think, understand and learn things quickly and well • *Susan's a very intelligent woman.*

odd ADJECTIVE
strange or unusual • *His behaviour was odd.*

organize VERB
to plan or arrange something • *We decided to organize a concert.*

plump ADJECTIVE
round and rather heavy • *Maria was small and plump.*

prepare VERB
to get ready for an event • *You should begin to prepare for the cost of your child's education.*

run VERB
to be in charge of a business or an activity • *She runs a restaurant in San Francisco.*

strange ADJECTIVE
unusual or unexpected • *There was something strange about the way she spoke.*

tattoo NOUN
a design on a person's skin made with a needle and coloured ink • *He has a tattoo on his arm.*

topic NOUN
a particular subject that you discuss or write about • *What is the topic of your essay?*

Unit 3

belong VERB
to be owned by someone • *The house has belonged to her family for three generations.*

borrow VERB
to use something that belongs to another person for a period of time and then return it • *Can I borrow a pen please?*

designer ADJECTIVE
expensive and fashionable because made by a famous designer • *I love your designer shoes, Julianna!*

flowing ADJECTIVE
hanging freely or loosely • *She wore a beautiful, flowing dress on the beach yesterday.*

leather NOUN
animal skin that is used for making shoes, clothes, bags and furniture • *Please don't spill any water on my leather couch.*

lend VERB
to allow someone to use something of yours for a period of time • *Will you lend me your pen?*

move VERB
to go to live in a different place • *She's moving to Cornwall next month.*

old-fashioned ADJECTIVE
no longer used, done or believed by most people • *The kitchen was old-fashioned and in bad condition.*

pack VERB
to put clothes and other things into a bag, because you are going away • *I began to pack for the trip.*

resort NOUN
a place that provides activities for people who stay there during their holiday • *The ski resorts are busy.*

storage UNCOUNTABLE NOUN
when you keep something in a special place until it is needed • *This room is used for storage.*

vintage ADJECTIVE
old, but of good quality • *Vintages clothes are beautiful, but can be very expensive.*

Unit 4

block NOUN
a group of buildings in a town or a city with streets on all sides • *He walked around the block three times.*

disgusting ADJECTIVE
extremely unpleasant or unacceptable • *The food tasted disgusting.*

empty ADJECTIVE
used for describing a place or container that has no people or things in it • *There were empty cans all over the floor.*

hill NOUN
an area of land that is higher than the land around it • *The castle is on a hill above the old town.*

miss VERB
to not take part in a meeting or an activity • *He missed the party because he had to work.*

noisy ADJECTIVE
full of a lot of loud or unpleasant noise • *The airport was crowded and noisy.*

opposite ADVERB
across from • *He looked at the buildings opposite.*

packed ADJECTIVE
very full of people • *The shop was packed.*

skyscraper NOUN
a very tall building in a city • *There are lots of skyscrapers in New York City.*

terrible ADJECTIVE
extremely bad • *I have a terrible singing voice.*

trip NOUN
a journey that you make to a particular place and back again • *She has just returned from a trip to Switzerland.*

unsafe ADJECTIVE
dangerous; not safe • *The water here is unsafe to drink.*

Unit 5

attend VERB
to be present at an event • *Thousands of people attended the wedding.*

board meeting NOUN
when a group of people who control a company meet to discuss the company • *The board meeting takes place every month.*

cancel VERB
to say that something that has been planned will not happen • *We cancelled our trip to Washington.*

celebrate VERB
to do something enjoyable for a special reason • *I passed my test and wanted to celebrate.*

diary NOUN
a book with a separate space for each day of the year that you use to write down things that you plan to do, or to record what happens in your life • *I read the entry in his diary for July 10, 1940.*

directions PLURAL NOUN
instructions that tell you what to do, how to do something, or how to get somewhere • *She stopped the car to ask for directions.*

finalise VERB
to make complete • *They have two days to finalise their orders.*

interview NOUN
a formal meeting in which someone asks you questions to find out if you are the right person for a job • *The interview went well, so I hope that I've got the job.*

offer VERB
to ask someone if they would like to have something • *He offered his seat to the young woman.*

pick up VERB
to collect someone or something from a place, often in a car • *Please could you pick me up at 5pm?*

postpone VERB
to arrange for an event to happen at a later time • *He decided to postpone the trip until the following day.*

to give someone a ring VERB
to make a telephone call to somebody • *We'll give him a ring later.*

Unit 6

code NOUN
a set of instructions that a computer can understand • *...a few lines of simple computer code.*

form NOUN
a piece of paper with questions on it and spaces where you should write the answers • *Please fill in this form and sign it at the bottom.*

hand in VERB
to take something to someone and give it to them • *I need to hand in my homework today.*

home NOUN
the house or flat where someone lives • *Hi, Mum, I'm home!*

mobile NOUN
a telephone that you can carry wherever you go • *The woman called the police on her mobile.*

move VERB
to put something in a different place • *A police officer asked him to move his car.*

online ADVERB
connected to the Internet. Compare with offline • *I buy most of my clothes online.*

park VERB
to stop a vehicle and leave it somewhere • *They parked their car in the street outside the house.*

printer NOUN
a machine for printing copies of computer documents on paper • *I need to buy some more paper for my printer.*

reserved ADJECTIVE
when something is kept specially for that person • *This table is reserved for us.*

suitcase NOUN
a case for carrying your clothes when you are travelling • *It did not take Andrew long to pack a suitcase.*

take a photo PHRASE
to make a picture using a camera • *Betty took a photo of us.*

Unit 7

book VERB
to arrange to have or use something, such as a hotel room or a ticket to a concert, at a later time • *Laurie booked a flight home.*

cash NOUN
money in the form of notes and coins • *Would you like to pay with cash?*

deposit NOUN
a sum of money that is part of the full price of something, and that you pay when you agree to buy it • *He paid a £500 deposit for the car.*

to have in VERB
to eat or drink something on the premises • *Would you like your coffee to have in or take away?*

pastry NOUN
a small cake • *The bakery sells delicious cakes and pastries.*

PIN NOUN
a secret number which you can use, for example, with a bank card to withdraw money from a cash machine • *I always forget the PIN for my bank card!*

receipt NOUN
a piece of paper that shows that you have received goods or money from someone • *I gave her a receipt for the money.*

reserve VERB
to keep something for a particular person or purpose • *I have reserved a table for this evening.*

stadium NOUN
a large sports pitch with rows of seats all around it • *The football match is taking place in a stadium.*

take away NOUN
to eat or drink something off the premises • *I'm in a hurry, so I will have my coffee to take away!*

VIP seats PLURAL NOUN
the best and most expensive seats in a venue. VIP stands for 'Very Important Person'. • *It's my birthday, so I booked VIP seats for us at the cinema!*

Unit 8

abbreviation NOUN
a short form of a word or phrase • *The abbreviation for 'page' is 'p.'*

acronym NOUN
a word made of the initial letters of the words in a phrase • *NATO is an acronym of 'North Atlantic Treaty Organization'.*

appointment NOUN
an arrangement to see someone at a particular time • *She has an appointment with her doctor.*

contract NOUN
an official agreement between two companies or two people • *He signed a contract to play for the team for two years.*

internet provider NOUN
a company that provides Internet and email services • *Your local internet provider will help you if you can't get access to the Internet.*

landline NOUN
the phone you have in your house, as opposed to your mobile phone • *I use my landline to phone my family in France because it's cheaper than using my mobile phone.*

one-off payment NOUN
a single payment that you sometimes have to make when you sign a contract • *Sally had to make a one-off payment for three months when she signed a year-long contract with her local gym.*

opportunity NOUN
a situation in which it is possible for you to do something that you want to do • *I had an opportunity to go to New York and study.*

reception NOUN
the strength of the signal you get on your mobile phone • *I'm not able to phone my friend because the reception in here is very bad.*

salon NOUN
a place where you go to have your hair cut, or to have beauty treatments • *The club has a beauty salon and two swimming pools.*

Skype® NOUN
software application that allows users to make voice and video calls over the Internet • *I often use Skype to speak to my friends in Spain.*

Unit 9

dentist NOUN
a person whose job is to examine and treat people's teeth • *Visit your dentist twice a year for a checkup.*

early ADVERB
before the usual time • *I had to get up early this morning.*

emigrate VERB
to leave your own country and go to live in another country • *His parents emigrated to the U.S. in 1954.*

financial firm NOUN
a company that provides help with matters relating to money • *My financial firm advises me on how best to spend my money.*

graduate NOUN
a student who has completed a course at a college or university • *His parents are both college graduates. They studied at Cornell.*

offer NOUN
something that someone says they will give you or do for you • *I hope you will accept my offer of help.*

operation NOUN
when a doctor cuts open a patient's body in order to remove, replace or repair a part • *Charles had an operation on his arm.*

in a rush PHRASE
quickly • *The men left in a rush.*

serious ADJECTIVE
very bad; making people worried or afraid • *Crime is a serious problem in our society.*

stop NOUN
a place where buses or trains regularly stop so that people can get on and off • *Ann started to walk towards the bus stop.*

scholarship NOUN
money to help you to continue studying • *He won a scholarship to the Pratt Institute of Art.*

volunteer NOUN
someone who does work without being paid, because they want to do it • *She helps in a local school as a volunteer.*

Unit 10

better ADJECTIVE
of a higher standard than something else • *This book is better than her last one.*

cable car ADJECTIVE
a cabin suspended from and moved by an overhead cable • *Let's wait for the next cable car to take us to the top of the mountain.*

disgusting ADJECTIVE
extremely unpleasant or unacceptable • *The food tasted disgusting.*

enthusiastic ADJECTIVE
showing how much you like or enjoy something • *Tom was not very enthusiastic about the idea.*

flatmate NOUN
a person you share a flat with • *I live with two other flatmates and we get along really well.*

homesick ADJECTIVE
feeling unhappy because you are away from home and missing your family and friends • *He was homesick for his family.*

horrible ADJECTIVE
very unpleasant • *It was a horrible experience.*

keen on (something) PHRASE
liking someone or something a lot • *I'm not keen on physics and chemistry.*

knowledgeable ADJECTIVE
knowing a lot about a particular subject • *Our staff are all extremely knowledgeable about our products.*

ride NOUN
a trip on a horse or a bicycle, or in a vehicle • *She took some friends for a ride in the car.*

seminar NOUN
a class at a college or university in which the teacher and a small group of students discuss a topic • *Students are asked to prepare material for the weekly seminars.*

tourist NOUN
a person who is visiting a place on holiday • *About 75,000 tourists visit the town each year.*

Unit 11

company NOUN
a business that sells goods or services • *Her mother works for an insurance company.*

concentrate VERB
to give something all your attention • *He should concentrate on his studies.*

delivery NOUN
when someone brings letters, packages or other goods to a particular place • *Please allow 28 days for delivery of your order.*

go crazy PHRASE
to be extremely bored or upset, or feel that you cannot wait for something any longer • *Annie thought she might go crazy if she didn't find out soon.*

impossible ADJECTIVE
unable to be done or to happen • *The snow made it impossible to play the game.*

journey NOUN
an occasion when you travel from one place to another • *Their journey took them from Paris to Brussels.*

register VERB
to put your name on an official list, in order to be able to do a particular thing • *Thousands of people registered to vote.*

revise VERB
to study something again in order to prepare for an exam • *I have to revise for my maths exam.*

revision NOUN
the process of rereading a subject or notes on it, especially in preparation for an examination • *I have so much revision to do for the exams next week!*

shout VERB
to say something very loudly • *Andrew ran out of the house, shouting for help.*

software NOUN
computer programs • *He writes computer software.*

spreadsheet NOUN
a computer program that deals with numbers • *I used a spreadsheet to calculate how much money I've spent on new clothes this month.*

Unit 12

advice NOUN
what you say to someone when you are telling them what you think they should do • *Take my advice and stay away from him!*

appreciate VERB
to be grateful for something that someone has done for you • *Peter helped me so much. I really appreciate that.*

busy ADJECTIVE
working hard, so that you are not free to do anything else • *What is it? I'm busy.*

calm down VERB
to become less upset or excited • *Calm down and listen to me.*

nephew NOUN
the son of your sister or brother • *I am planning a birthday party for my nephew.*

online ADVERB
connected to the Internet • *You can chat to other people online.*

penalty NOUN
a punishment for doing something that is against a law or rule • *The maximum penalty for dangerous driving is five years in prison.*

promotion NOUN
when you are given a more important job or rank in the organization that you work for • *I got a promotion after three years of being an assistant for the company. Now I'm a manager!*

struggle VERB
to try hard to do something that you find very difficult • *She struggled to find the right words.*

submit VERB
to formally send something to someone, so that they can consider it • *They submitted their reports yesterday.*

unpack VERB
to take things out of a suitcase or a box • *He unpacked his bag.*

vacancy NOUN
a job that has not been filled • *We have a vacancy for an assistant.*

Unit 13

board VERB
to get into a train, a ship or an aircraft to travel somewhere • *I boarded the plane to Boston.*

delay VERB
to make someone or something late • *Our flight was delayed for three hours.* NOUN when something does not happen until later than planned or expected • *He apologized for the delay.*

exchange NOUN
anything given or received as a replacement for something else • *My new jumper didn't fit so I took it back to the shop to get an exchange.*

flight NOUN
a trip in an aircraft • *Our flight was two hours late.*

fresh ADJECTIVE
done, made or experienced recently • *There were fresh car tracks in the snow.*

investigate VERB
to try to find out how something happened • *Police are investigating how the accident happened.*

receipt NOUN
a piece of paper that shows that you have received goods or money from someone • *I gave her a receipt for the money.*

refund NOUN
money that is returned to you because you have paid too much, or because you have returned goods to a shop • *He took the boots back to the shop and asked for a refund.*

repair VERB
to fix something that has been damaged or is not working properly • *He has repaired the roof.*

screen NOUN
a flat surface on a piece of electronic equipment, such as a television or a computer, where you see pictures or words • *My computer screen isn't working, so I'm unable to write any emails at the moment.*

voucher NOUN
a piece of paper that can be used instead of money to pay for something • *As a birthday present, John gave Sally a voucher for a pair of cinema tickets.*

warranty NOUN
a promise by a company that if you buy something that does not work, they will repair it or replace it • *The TV comes with a twelve-month warranty.*

Unit 14

ago ADVERB
in the past; before now • *I got your letter a few days ago.*

disturb VERB
to interrupt someone or something by talking to them or making a noise • *Only the occasional passing car disturbed the silence.*

embarrassed ADJECTIVE
feeling shy, ashamed or guilty about something • *He looked a bit embarrassed when he noticed his mistake.*

fall out PHRASE to have an argument with someone and stop being friendly with them • *Ashley has fallen out with her boyfriend.*

grumpy ADJECTIVE
a little angry • *He's getting grumpy and depressed.*

miss VERB
to not take part in a meeting or an activity • *He missed the party because he had to work.* to feel sad because someone is no longer with you, or because you no longer have the thing • *Your mother and I are going to miss you at Christmas.*

presentation NOUN
an occasion when someone shows or explains something to a group of people • *Philip and I gave a short presentation.*

regret VERB
to feel sorry that you did something • *I regret my decision to leave my job.*

rude ADJECTIVE
not polite • *He's so rude to her friends.*

tired ADJECTIVE
feeling that you want to rest or sleep • *Michael is tired after his long flight.*

upset VERB
to make you feel worried or unhappy • *What you said in your letter really upset me.*

Unit 15

accident NOUN
when a vehicle hits something and causes injury or damage • *He broke his right leg in a motorbike accident.* NOUN when something bad happens to a person by chance, sometimes causing injury or death • *The boy was injured in an accident at a swimming pool.*

dangerous ADJECTIVE
able or likely to harm you • *We are in a very dangerous situation.*

fault NOUN
if something bad is your fault, you made it happen • *The accident was my fault.*

imagine VERB
to form a picture or idea of something in your mind • *He could not imagine a more peaceful scene.*

lose control PHRASE
to stop being able to make something do what you want it to do • *I lost control of my bike and fell.*

nervous ADJECTIVE
frightened or worried • *I was very nervous during the job interview.*

painful ADJECTIVE
hurting • *Her toe was swollen and painful.*

safe ADJECTIVE
not in danger • *Where's Sophie? Is she safe?*

shuttle bus NOUN
a plane, bus, or train that makes regular trips between two places • *There is a free shuttle between the airport terminals.*

ski VERB
to move over snow or water on long, flat, narrow pieces of wood, metal or plastic that you fasten to your boots • *They tried to ski down Mount Everest.*

take care PHRASE to look after someone • *There was no one to take care of the children.*

terrified ADJECTIVE
extremely afraid • *I'm terrified of flying.*

Unit 16

busy ADJECTIVE
working hard, so that you are not free to do anything else • *They are busy preparing for a party on Saturday.*

change NOUN
the money that you get back when you pay with more money than something costs • *'There's your change.'—'Thanks very much.'*

delicious ADJECTIVE
very good to eat • *There was a wide choice of delicious meals.*

gift NOUN
something that you give to someone as a present • *We gave her a birthday gift.*

glad ADJECTIVE
happy and pleased about something • *They seemed glad to see me.*

heavy ADJECTIVE
weighing a lot • *This bag is very heavy. What's in it?*

pass VERB
to give an object to someone • *Pam passed the books to Dr Wong.*

picnic NOUN
when you eat a meal outdoors, usually in a park or a forest, or at the beach • *I took the kids for a picnic.*

shame NOUN
something that you feel sad or disappointed about • *It was a shame about the weather, but the party was still a great success.*

starving ADJECTIVE
very hungry • *Does anyone have any food? I'm starving.*

watch NOUN
a small clock that you wear on your wrist • *Dan gave me a watch for my birthday.*

Unit 17

accommodation NOUN
buildings or rooms where people live or stay • *They always pay extra for luxury accommodation.*

apply VERB
to write a letter or write on a form in order to ask for something such as a job • *I am applying for a new job.*

artist NOUN
someone who draws, paints or creates other works of art • *Each painting is signed by the artist.*

exhibition NOUN
a public event where art or interesting objects are shown • *The Museum of the City of New York has an exhibition of photographs.*

improve VERB
to get better • *Their French improved during their trip to Paris.*

interview NOUN
a formal meeting in which someone asks you questions to find out if you are the right person for a job • *The interview went well, so I hope that I've got the job.*

painting NOUN
a picture that someone has painted • *She hung a large painting on the wall.*

qualification NOUN
an examination result or a skill that you need to be able to do something • *I believe I have all the qualifications to be a good teacher.*

residential course NOUN
a course that requires you to live in the same place where you are studying • *Taking a residential course is a great way to make new friends.*

talk NOUN
when someone speaks to a group of people • *She gave a brief talk on the history of the building.*

training NOUN
the process of learning the skills that you need for a particular job or activity • *Kennedy had no formal training as an artist.*

visa NOUN
an official document or a stamp in your passport that allows you to enter a particular country.

worried ADJECTIVE
thinking about problems that you have or about unpleasant things that might happen • *He seemed very worried.*

Unit 18

air pollution NOUN
chemicals or other substances that have a harmful effect on the air • *We think that air pollution may be the cause of the illness.*

cheating NOUN
the act of not obeying a set of rules, for example in a game or exam • *James was accused of cheating during his exam.*

fuel NOUN
a substance such as coal or oil that is burned to provide heat or power • *They bought some fuel on the motorway.*

generation NOUN
all the people in a group or country who are of a similar age • *The current generation of teens are the richest in history.*

green ADJECTIVE
relating to the protection of the environment • *Recycling paper is green.*

module NOUN
one of the units that some university or college courses are divided into • *These courses cover a twelve-week period and are organised into three four-week modules.*

part-time ADJECTIVE
working for only part of each day or week • *She is trying to get a part-time job in an office.*

responsibility NOUN
to have the job of dealing with something or someone • *Each manager had responsibility for ten people.*

run VERB
to be in charge of a business or an activity • *She runs a restaurant in San Francisco.*

tuition fees PLURAL NOUN
money that you have to pay for being taught in a university.

unsocial hours PLURAL NOUN
hours of work of some jobs that fall outside the normal working day • *Being a doctor means I sometimes work unsocial hours, for example very late at night.*

waste VERB
to use too much of something such as time, money or energy doing something that is not important • *I decided not to waste money on a hotel room.*

smart ADJECTIVE
right for a formal occasion or activity; clean and tidy • *He looked very smart in his new uniform.*

style NOUN
the way that someone usually dresses • *This long dress isn't my style as I prefer short dresses.*

suitcase NOUN
a case for carrying your clothes when you are travelling • *It did not take Andrew long to pack a suitcase.*

ugly ADJECTIVE
very unpleasant to look at • *The museum is a rather ugly building.*

unwanted ADJECTIVE
not wanted or loved • *Delete unwanted emails from your computer.*

Unit 19

close VERB
to shut a door or a window • *If you are cold, close the window.*

disturb VERB to interrupt someone or something by talking to them or making a noise • *Only the occasional passing car disturbed the silence.*

fair ADJECTIVE
reasonable, right, and just • *It didn't seem fair to ignore her father.*

mind VERB
used when you are happy to do or have either of two choices • *'Would you rather play tennis or baseball?' — 'I don't mind.'*

old-fashioned ADJECTIVE
no longer used, done or believed by most people • *The kitchen was old-fashioned and in bad condition.*

private ADJECTIVE
only for one particular person or group, and not for everyone • *It was a private conversation, so I'm not going to talk about it to anyone else.*

return VERB
to give back or put back something that you borrowed or took • *They will return the money later.*

Unit 20

applicant NOUN
someone who formally asks to be considered for a job or a course • *The company keeps records on every job applicant.*

congratulate VERB
to express pleasure about something good that has happened to someone • *She congratulated him on the birth of his son.*

date NOUN
a particular day and month or a particular year • *'What's the date today?' — '23rd July.'*

deserve VERB
to be worthy of something because of your actions or qualities • *These people deserve to get more money.*

invite VERB
to ask someone to come to an event • *She invited him to her 26th birthday party.*

mall NOUN
a large building with lots of shops and restaurants inside it • *I'm going to the mall with some friends to go shopping and have some lunch.*

online ADVERB
connected to the Internet • *You can chat to other people online.*

organize VERB
to plan or arrange something • *We decided to organize a concert.*

over the moon PHRASE
used to say that you are very pleased about something
• *Samantha is over the moon that she got the job!*

pick (somebody) up PHRASE
to collect someone or something from a place, often in a
car • *Please could you pick me up at 5pm?*

proud ADJECTIVE
pleased and satisfied about something good that you or
other people close to you have done • *His dad was very
proud of him.*

relief NOUN
when you feel happy because something unpleasant has
not happened or is no longer happening
• *I breathed a sigh of relief.*

ANSWER KEY

Unit 1   Meeting people

Conversations

1

Know each other: 1, 3
Meeting for the first time: 2, 4

2

1	Clare	5	Andy
2	Sarah	6	Karen
3	Mr Williams	7	Tina
4	Sam (Jones)	8	Mark

3

1	Lovely	4	too	7	news
2	Pleased	5	introduce	8	journey
3	Nice	6	know	9	finding

Saying it accurately

1

1 let   2 this   3 Pleased   4 too

2–3

1 Gary: Hi Paul, it's great to see you.
2 Paul: Hiya, you too. How are things?
3 Gary: Good, thanks. How are you doing?
4 Paul: I'm very well, thanks. How was your journey?
5 Gary: OK, thanks. The train was on time.

Saying it clearly

3

(Answers will vary. Suggested answers only)
1 Great, thanks.
2 Nice to meet you.
3 Good, thanks.
4 I'm getting married!

Saying it appropriately

1

1 a
2 2
3 2
4 1
5 2
6 2
7 1
8 1

Get speaking

1

1 b
2 d
3 a
4 c

Unit 2   Describing people

Conversations

1

a Positive and negative
b Negative
c Negative
d Negative
e Positive

2

personality		appearance	
1	a good laugh	1	kind of tall
2	very intelligent	2	looks a bit odd
3	a funny bunch	3	kind of short
4	a know-it-all	4	a bit plump
5	a name-dropper	5	smiley
6	complete control freak		
7	two-faced		
8	has a heart of gold		

Saying it accurately

1

1	complete control freak	5	a funny bunch
2	very intelligent	6	good laugh
3	name-dropper	7	two-faced
4	a heart of gold	8	a know-it-all

2

1	a bit odd	4	kind of tall
2	smiley	5	kind of short
3	a bit plump		

Saying it clearly

2–3

3 **a** heart_of gold

4 kind_**of** tall

5 looks_**a** bit odd

Saying it appropriately

1–2

1 She is a <u>complete</u> control freak. She checks <u>everything</u>.

2 Carol has a <u>heart</u> of <u>gold</u>. She's <u>really</u> kind.

3 Tanya is <u>smiley</u>, but she's two-faced.

4 She's a <u>bit</u> plump.

3

(Answers will vary.)

Get speaking

1

(Answers will vary. Suggested answers only)

1 That's Dave. He's a bit plump and he's wearing a big hat. He's a know-it-all. He thinks he knows everything!

2 Ana is very smiley and she has a heart of gold. I was really worried about my exams last year and she helped me revise and stay positive.

3 My sister worked with them last summer. They're a funny bunch. They are all two-faced. They were very friendly to my sister and then said horrible things about her when she left the job.

4 They're nice actually. They're a good laugh and they are all very intelligent. They are all going to a top university next year.

Unit 3 Talking about things

Conversations

1

a	2	b	1	c	3

2

1	bits and bobs	8	loads of
2	stuff	9	lots of
3	things	10	many
4	greeny	11	much
5	kind of	12	hundreds
6	sort of	13	tonnes
7	pretty		

Saying it accurately

1

1

   1 many

   2 hundreds

   3 borrow

   4 silvery

2

   1 stuff

   2 tonnes

3 some things

4 kind

Saying it clearly

1–2

1 weak (unstressed)

2 weak (unstressed)

3 weak (unstressed)

4 weak (unstressed)

3

(Answers will vary.)

Saying it appropriately

1–2

1 pretty; old

2 tonnes; bags

3 hundreds; books

4 pretty; good

3

1 2

2 1

3 1

4 2

Get speaking

1

(Answers will vary. Suggested answers only)

1   Some old photos, a few books, and bits and bobs.

2   It's pretty old. It belonged to my grandmother.

3   I've got hundreds of pairs of shoes.

4   My coat. It's a bluey colour and it's really warm.

5   I've got tonnes of English textbooks.

Unit 4   Talking about places

1

how to find a place: 1, 4, 5

describing places: 2, 3

2

1

a taxi rank

Mr Kay's office

a good restaurant

2

positive: beautiful, amazing, great

negative: noisy, unsafe, packed, terrible, disgusting

3

You know the Empire State building?

The really high skyscraper?

You know where the big meeting room is?

Saying it accurately

1

1   Can you see the cafe on the corner?

2   Do you know the Empire State building?

3   Is that the really high skyscraper?

4   Do you know where the big meeting room is?

2–3

1   The big park in the centre of town?

2   You know Trafalgar Square?

3   You know where the canteen is?

4   You see the park at the end of the street?

Saying it appropriately

1

1 ✓		4 ✓
2 ✗		5 ✗
3 ✓		6 ✗

Get speaking

1

(Answers will vary.)

2   OK, You know where the shopping centre is? Go past the shopping centre, turn right, and the entrance to the train station is on the left. You can't miss it.

3   Let me think. You see the glass building at the end of the street? Go past that and turn left into a small square. There are two or three good cafés there.

Unit 5   Making arrangements

Conversations

1

a 2   b 3   c 1   d 4

2–3

	1	2	3	4
event	*Fancy coming round for dinner tonight?*	Is it still OK for you to pick me up tomorrow?	Would you be able to attend on Friday or Monday?	Are you still free for lunch today?
time	*Let's say 7 p.m.?*	Is 5.30 OK? The traffic can be be bad at that time.	Shall we say Friday at 10 a.m.?	
response	*Great, see you later*	Yeah, good point. I'll pick you up at 5 pm then.	Look forward to seeing you then.	I'm running late. Can we make it tomorrow?

Saying it accurately

1

1	for	4	at	7	for
2	to	5	to		
3	on	6	up		

2

1	b	3	a
2	d	4	c

Saying it appropriately

1–3

speaker 5 sounds sorry

Get speaking

2

(Answers will vary. Suggested answers only)

1   Is it still OK for you to pick me up?
2   About six. Is that OK?
3   Thanks. See you later.

3

1   Sorry, I'm running late. Can we make it tomorrow?
2   Great, thank you. See you tomorrow.

4

1   I can make Wednesday.
2   Yes, that's fine.
3   And you, thanks. Bye.

Unit 6   Making requests

Conversations

1

(Answers will vary.)

3

1	indirect	5	indirect
2	indirect	6	direct
3	indirect	7	indirect
4	direct		

4

formal

1   Excuse me, would you mind taking our photo?
2   Do you mind if I hand in the essay on Monday?
3   Could you possibly explain that again please?
4   Excuse me, is it ok if I park my car here?
5   Is it OK if I go to the cinema with Cathy tonight?

informal

1   Could you move your coat please?
2   Can I use your mobile?

Saying it accurately

1

1	possibly	3	if	5	OK
2	Can	4	you	6	mind

2

1	helping	5	pass
2	give	6	pay
3	tell	7	use
4	I call		

Saying it clearly

1–2

1   <u>Excuse</u> me, would you mind taking our <u>photo</u>?
2   Could you possibly explain that <u>again</u> please?
3   Do you mind if I hand in the essay <u>on Monday</u>?
4   Is it OK if I go <u>to the cinema</u> with Cathy tonight?
5   Can I use <u>your</u> mobile?
6   Could you <u>move</u> your coat, please?

Saying it appropriately

1–3

1   Impolite
2   Polite
3   Impolite
4   Polite
5   Impolite
6   Polite

Get speaking

1

(Answers will vary. Suggested answers only)

1   Is it OK if I go to Terry's house tonight?
2   Excuse me, is it OK if I sit here?
3   Can I borrow your book, Andy?
4   Could you move your bag please?
5   Could you possibly explain that again, please?
6   Do you mind if I hand in the homework next week?

Unit 7   Ordering and buying

Conversations

1

Conversation 2

2

1   False (afternoon course)
2   True (the course is £350)
3   True
4   False (6.30 p.m.)
5   True
6   False (credit/debit card)
7   True
8   False (black coffee and chocolate cookie)

3

1

I'd like to reserve
Can I have a
Do you have any
Can I get?
Could I book
How much does ... cost?

2

Let me see
Let me think

3

That sounds good
That's very expensive

4

I'll take those please.
I'll pay now please.

Saying it accurately

1–2

a	2	f	1
b	5	g	7
c	9	h	4
d	6	i	8
e	3		

Saying it clearly

1

1	£20	3	£50
2	£4.50	4	£100

extra: £4.15, 20p

2–3

1   six pounds and fifteen pence; six, fifteen
2   eighty quid; eighty pounds
3   one-hundred pounds; a hundred pounds
4   seven, fifty; seven pounds and fifty pence

4–5

1   seven, forty-five; quarter to eight
2   half past six; six-thirty
3   nine; nine (a.m. / p.m.); nine o'clock

Saying it appropriately

1–2

1   Let me see, OK, that sounds good.
2   Let me think, I'll take those, please.

3–4

1   Let_me see. OK, that sounds good.
2   Let_me think. I'll take those please.
3   Do_you have_any tickets for tonight's film?

Get speaking

1

(Answers will vary. Suggested answers only)

1

• Hello, I'd like to reserve a place on next week's English course, please.
• Great. How much does it cost?
• That sounds good.
• I'll pay now please.

2

• Do you have any tickets left for the concert?
• Great. How much are they?
• That's very expensive. I'll take three £50 tickets, please.

3

• Can I get a coffee, please?
• Let me see. I'll have a cake, please.
• To go, please.

Unit 8   Speaking on the phone

Conversations

1

a   Dan

b   Lisa Evans

c   Mr Dawson

d   1

2

1   Sorry I can't take your call

2   I'll get back to you as soon as I can.

3   I'm just calling to say

4   the line's terrible

5   Can you repeat that?

6   I didn't catch that.

7   Yes, speaking.

8   Listen, I'm not interested.

Saying it accurately

1

1 take	5 Listen
2 get	6 hear
3 get	7 catch
4 speak	8 line

Saying it clearly

1

Speaker B is clear and easy to understand.

Speaker A speaks too quickly and does not leave pauses between phrases.

3

(Answers will vary.)

Saying it appropriately

1

1   er / uh

2   um

3   mmm

4   (sigh)

Get speaking

1

(Answers will vary. Suggested answers only)

1

- Hey, how are you? Do you want to come round for dinner this week?
- Which day is OK for you?
- Call me when you get this message, then we can arrange things. OK? Bye.

2

- Yes, the line's terrible. It's difficult to hear you.
- Sorry, can you repeat that?
- OK. Shall we meet at 6.30 at your house?

3

- er… umm… Thank you, but I'm not interested.
- er… umm… No, I'm sorry, I'm really not interested.
- (sigh) Listen, I'm not interested. Thank you for calling. Goodbye.

Unit 9   Showing interest in a conversation

Conversations

1

Conversation 1 and Conversation 4

2

Who?

Not Geoff?

Really… so what did he say?

He was such a nice teacher, wasn't he?

3

Really?

What are they?

What's the other job?

4

Short exclamations to show interest

Really?

No way!

Wow!

Phrases to conclude a conversation

Sorry, I'm afraid, I have to go.

I'm in a rush. I have to be at

I'd love to chat but I have to

Sorry. I better get going.

I really have to go.

Saying it accurately

1

1	way	3	really
2	rush	4	better

2

3 Guess what? I've got a place at two universities!

5 Wow! Well done. Which ones?

1 One is here in London. They gave me a scholarship too!

4 No way! That's great. Where's the other one?

2 In America at the same university my sister goes to.

Saying it clearly

1

1 to

2 a

3 to, at, the

4 to, to

2

1 I have to go.

2 I'm in a rush.

3 I have to be at the doctor's at 10.

4 I'd love to chat but I have to go.

Saying it appropriately

1

1	a
2	b
3	a

Get speaking

1

(Answers will vary. Suggested answers only).

1

- Mmmm.
- Right.
- This is my stop. I have to go.

2

- Really? Well done! What are they?
- No way! That's great.
- Wow! They both sound great.

3

- Not really. I'd love to chat, but I've got an appointment.
- Sorry, I've got an appointment with the dentist. I better get going. I'm catching a bus in five minutes.

Unit 10   Developing a conversation

Conversations

1

a	3	b	4	c	2	d	1

2

1	really good	6	great
2	horrible	7	nice
3	very hard	8	And very enthusiastic.
4	I feel homesick too.	9	delicious
5	terrible		

Saying it accurately

1

1	too	3	neither	5	like
2	difficult	4	Really	6	Terrible

Saying it clearly

1

amazing = 3

difficult = 3

exciting = 3

friendly = 2

handsome = 2

interesting = 3

knowledgeable = 4

seminar = 3

terrible = 3

2

O o	handsome
	friendly
O o o	difficult
	terrible
	seminar
	interesting
o O o	exciting
	amazing
O o o o	knowledgeable

Get speaking

1

(Answers will vary. Suggested answers only)

1

- No, me neither.
- Terrible. It was very cold.
- Yeah, me too. They were really nice.

2

- Amazing!
- Me too. I'm very excited.
- Really good. And very intelligent.

Unit 11   Checking for understanding

Conversations

1

a 3   b 1   c 2   d 4

2

1 *Don't get me wrong.*
2 What I'm trying to say is
3 What I mean is
4 You mean
5 *See what I mean?*
6 You know
7 Does that make sense?
8 Know what I mean?
9 *What do you mean?*
10 What are you saying?
11 Is that right?
12 Got it!
13 I see.
14 Sorry, I don't get you.

Saying it accurately

1

1 Don't   4 Know / See
2 What   5 Does
3 What   6 Sorry

2

1 Explaining something again
2 Explaining something again
3 Explaining something again
4 Checking someone understands me
5 Checking someone understands me
6 Saying I don't understand

Saying it appropriately

3

1 Know what I <u>mean</u>?
2 Does that make <u>sense</u>?
3 <u>What</u> are you <u>saying</u>?

Get speaking

1 (Answers will vary. Suggested answers only).

1

- Click the green button. Enter my password. Is that right?
- OK, got it! Thanks.

2

- You just need to make a study diary.
- Look at my study diary. Today I'm studying Maths and Science. Tomorrow is a day off. On Wednesday, I'm writing a draft for my English essay.

Unit 12   Listening to problems

Conversations

1

a 1   b 3   c 2

2

1 doesn't enjoy her job; look for another job
2 time management; go on a time management course
3 Julie's mum worrying about Julie going to college; visit Aunt Sue

3

suggestions	responses
Why don't you ... ? 1	That sounds great. 1
You need to 1	Thanks for listening to me. 1
You should 1	That sounds like a great idea! 2
If I were you, I'd 1	I really appreciate your help. 2
We need to 2	That's a good plan. 3
You should 2	
You should 3	
Why don't you ... ? 3	

Saying it accurately

1

1 should   3 were

2 need   4 don't

2

1 I really appreciate your help.

2 It's a complicated situation.

3 That sounds like a great idea.

4 I don't know what to do.

5 I feel really confused.

6 Thanks for listening to me.

7 I'm struggling with my course.

3

1, 3, 6

Saying it clearly

1

1 <u>It's</u> difficult.

2 <u>I'm</u> struggling.

3 <u>I'd</u> buy a newspaper.

4 <u>That's</u> not fair.

5 <u>What's</u> up?

6 Why <u>don't</u> you call her? (negative contraction)

Saying it appropriately

1

To help them feel better

Get speaking

1

(Answers will vary. Suggested answers only)

1

- Oh dear. Why don't you talk to another teacher and ask for help?
- OK, OK, calm down. If I were you, I'd speak to another teacher first. Then we can talk to mum and dad together.

2

- Everything's fine, Mum. I've got everything.
- Don't worry, Mum. You don't; need to worry. I'll call you when I get there.

Unit 13   Making a complaint

Conversations

1

a 3

b 2

c 1

2

1 False

2 True

3 True

4 True

5 False (steak)

6 False (45 minutes)

7 False (The manager isn't here today.)

3

Making a complaint

1 There seems to be a problem

2 That's not good enough.

3 I'm sorry, but

4 I don't want to make a fuss but

5 I'm phoning to complain about

6 The first problem was that

Responding to a complaint

1 Oh dear.

2 I'm very sorry about that

3 Can I offer you a

4 Oh, I'm sorry to hear that.

5 I'm so sorry we let you down.

Saying it accurately

1

1 e   5 b

2 c   6 f

3 a   7 d

4 g

2

strongest: 1 e

most polite: 7d

Saying it clearly

1

unstressed (weak); the schwa sound / ə /

3

Saying it appropriately

1

1 a
2 b
3 b
4 a
5 a

Get speaking

1

(Answers will vary. Suggested answers only)

1

- Hello, I bought this cell phone last week, but there seems to be a problem. It stopped working yesterday.
- I'd like an exchange please.
- Yes, here you are.

2

- Sorry, but we didn't order this. My friend ordered the steak.
- Actually, I don't think my food looks cooked.
- I'm really disappointed. This is terrible.
- We're leaving. Come on, let's go.

Unit 14   Making an apology

Conversations

1

1, 2, 4

2

1 Pete   3 Debs
2 Neil   4 James

3

terribly, really, so

The adverbs make the apology stronger.

4

1 *I wanted to apologise for*
2 I wanted to say sorry
3 *make up for*
4 make it up to
5 *I didn't want to upset you*
6 I really regret it.
7 I didn't mean it.
8 *Apology accepted.*
9 Let's forget about it.
10 I'm sorry to disturb you
11 I'm sorry I'm late.

Saying it accurately

1

1 I'm sorry to disturb you.
2 I didn't want to upset you.
3 Let's forget about it.
4 I'm sorry I'm late.
5 I didn't mean it.

2

1 for
2 to
3 over
4 about
5 up

3

1 Let's not fall out over it. It doesn't matter. (b)
2 You have to make up for arriving an hour late. (a)
3 I'm going to make it up to you. (c)

Saying it clearly

1

1 I <u>didn't</u> mean it.
2 I <u>didn't</u> want to upset you.
3 <u>Don't</u> worry.
4 You <u>didn't</u> even say sorry.
5 <u>I'm</u> sorry <u>I'm</u> late.

2

1 2
2 2
3 1
4 2
5 1, 1

Saying it appropriately

1

1 a   4 a
2 b   5 a
3 b   6 b

Get speaking

1

(Answers will vary. Suggested answers only).

1

- I know. I really regret it. I'm sorry.
- I didn't mean it. I had a long day at work yesterday and I was really tired. Can I make it up to you? Cook you dinner tonight?

2

- You're always late. It's freezing.
- OK. Let's forget about it.

3

- I'm sorry to disturb you. Do you have a minute?
- I wanted to apologise for missing the meeting this morning. I forgot the time of the meeting.

Unit 15   Showing sympathy

Conversations

1

a 3   b 4   c 2   d 1

2

1 It's my own fault.
2 I can imagine.
3 Oh, I'm sorry. Oh dear.
4 Cheer up. It's not the end of the world. It's not that bad.
5 That's awful! / How frightening!
6 That's good news. Why don't you try to... ? Call me if you need anything.
7 I know how you feel.
8 Try not to worry. Stay positive.

Saying it accurately

1

1 awful!   2 own   3 sorry

Extra: mind, worry

3

1 can   3 don't   5 know
2 's not   4 need   6 worry

Saying it appropriately

2

1 ✓   5 ✓
2 ✗   6 ✗
3 ✗   7 ✓
4 ✓

Get speaking

1

(Answers will vary. Suggested answers only)

1

- That's what friends are for. How are you feeling?
- I can imagine. You're safe now.

2

- Oh, I'm sorry. What happened?
- Oh dear. I think everybody makes mistake in tests. Try not to worry.

3

- I'm afraid you didn't get the new job in the department.
- I know how you feel. Stay positive. It takes a long time to get a new job.

Unit 16   Saying 'thank you'

Conversations

1

1	home	Aunt and niece/nephew
2	any place	friends
3	cafe/coffee stall	barista/server and customer
4	home	friends
5	office/place of work	colleagues/strangers
6	office/place of work	friends
7	bar/cafe	friends

2

2: I'm visiting my sister this weekend.
5: problem with my back

3

saying thanks to a friend

1 Cheers.
2 Thanks for
3 Thanks for asking

saying 'no thanks'

1 I'd love to but

saying thanks in a more formal situation

1   Thank you so much
2   I appreciate it.

responding to others saying thanks

1   No problem.
2   I'm glad you liked it.
3   You're welcome.
4   No worries.
5   That's OK.

Saying it accurately

1

1   a, b   2   b, c   3   b, c
2
1   I'd   3   I'm   5   That's
2   No   4   No

Saying it clearly

2

a   2   b   4   c   1   d   3

Saying it appropriately

1

friendly, genuine, polite

Get speaking

1

(Answers will vary. Suggested answers only)
1   Great. Thanks for helping me,
2   I love it. Thank you so much for the present.
3   I'd love to but I'm busy. Thanks for asking.

3

1   No problem.   3   You're welcome.
2   No worries.

Unit 17   Agreeing and disagreeing

Conversations

1

1   informal
2   Tony doesn't like him and thinks he's a bad actor.

2

3   different ages; informal
4   She's nervous and thinks there are problems.

	Conversation 1	Conversation 2
introduce a positive opinion	**1** Actually	
introduce a negative opinion	**2** To be honest	
explain your opinion 'isn't very important'	**3** I'm just saying **4** It's no big deal	
agree but then disagree	**5** Yeah, I know but	**6** Maybe, but **7** I suppose so, but **8** I know what you mean, but
repeat and expand your opinion		**9** You know **10** What I mean is

Saying it accurately

1

1   c   3   b
2   a
2
1   You know
2   I know what you mean, but
3   To be honest

Saying it clearly

1–2

You cannot hear the bold letters.

Saying it appropriately

1–2

positive 1
negative 5
neutral 2, 3, 4, 6, 7

Get speaking

1

(Answers will vary. Suggested answers only)

Conversation 1

1   Actually, I really liked the album.

2   Well, to be honest, I don't like that track.

3   I'm just saying. I don't like it. It's no big deal.

Conversation 2

4   What I mean is you have to write in a formal tone.

5   I know what you mean, but we studied formal and informal letters last semester. Do you remember?

Unit 18   Stronger opinions

Conversations

1

a

1   same opinion
2   different opinion
3   same opinion
4   different opinion

b

Rosa shows very strong disagreement.

2

Commenting on an opinion

1   Are you serious?
2   Excuse me?
3   How can you say that?
4   That's ridiculous!
5   You don't know what you're talking about!
6   Really? Do you think so?

Giving your opinion

1   No, let me stop you there.
2   Can I just say that...
3   What I'm trying to say is
4   Sorry to butt in
5   Yes, I get your point but...
6   What I will say is...

Concluding an agreement and disagreement

1   I think we're both saying the same thing.
2   You have your opinion and I have mine.
3   I can see your point.

Saying it accurately

1

1 f	3 a	5 b
2 c	4 e	6 d

Saying it clearly

2

1   Can I <u>just</u> say that...
2   What I <u>will</u> say is...

Saying it appropriately

2-3

1   <u>Excuse</u> me?
2   <u>No</u>, let me <u>stop</u> you there.
3   What I'm <u>trying</u> to say is...
4   Yes, I <u>get</u> your point but...
5   How can you <u>say</u> that?

Get speaking

1

(Answers will vary. Suggested answers only)

1

- How can you say that? The bus is better.
- Sorry, but the buses are late because there are too many cars on the road. Cars aren't good for the environment. Think about the fuel they use.
- Ok, I get your point. You have your opinion and I have mine.

2

- Are you serious?
- Let me stop you there. I'm studying hard because I need good grades and I want to get a scholarship at university.
- You have your opinion and I have mine.

Unit 19   Giving feedback

Conversations

1

a 3	e 2	
b 1	f 4	
c 3	g 4	
d 2	h 1	

2

Expressing an undecided opinion

1   *Well, I'm not sure.*

2   I hope so.

Giving your opinion

1   *It's a bit...*

2   If I were you, I would
3   I don't think it suits you.
4   It's not really me, to be honest.

Making a polite request
1   *Can I have a quick word?*
2   Could we talk about... ?
3   I wonder if you could...
4   Perhaps you should...

Saying it accurately

1
1   Can I have a quick word?
2   I wonder if you could close the door?
3   Perhaps you should try another dress?
4   Could we talk about your exam results?

3
1   try   3   improve
2   close   4   go

Saying it clearly

1
1   If I were you, I'd try another one.
2   I'm not sure.

3   I'd buy the black dress, if I were you.
4   It's a bit short.
5   I don't think it suits you.

Saying it appropriately

1
1   Mmm...
2   Um..., (pause)
3   Er...
4   um..., (pause)

Get speaking

1
(Answers will vary. Suggested answers only)
1
•   Well, I'm not sure.
•   I don't think it suits you. If I were you, I'd get an exchange.
2
•   Can I have a quick word?
•   I wonder if you could talk on your mobile outside.
•   Perhaps you could do it in another room. I'm trying to study for the exam.

Unit 20   Saying 'Well done!'

Conversations

1
a   2
b   4
c   1
d   3

2

Introducing good news
1   *Guess what?*
2   I've got something to tell you.
3   I wanted to invite you to...

Ways of saying 'well done!'
1   *Well done!*
2   *Congratulations!*
3   You deserve it.
4   I'm really pleased for you.
5   That's amazing!
6   That's wonderful news!
7   That's fantastic.
8   I'm proud of you.

Responses to 'well done'
1   *It's a big relief.*
2   *I can't believe it!*
3   I'm so excited.
4   I'm so happy.
5   Cheers.
6   Thanks.
7   That's really kind of you.

Saying it accurately

1
a   3   c   1
b   2   d   4

2
1   tell
2   to
3   for
4   of
5   it
6   of

Saying it clearly

1

O	pleased
	proud
O o o	wonderful
o O o	amazing
	excited
	fantastic
o o o O o	congratulations

Saying it appropriately

1

exclamation mark (!)

3

1	Speaker 1 J	Speaker 2 E
2	Speaker 1 E	Speaker 2 J
3	Speaker 1 E	Speaker 2 J

Get speaking

1

(Answers will vary. Suggested answers only)

- Well done!
- Congratulations! That's fantastic! I'm very proud of you.

2

- Guess what? I've got a new job!
- Thank you. I can't believe it.

3

- Congratulations! That's wonderful news!
- That's fantastic! How are you feeling? Are you nervous?

AUDIO SCRIPT

Unit 1   Meeting people

Track 01

(See pages 8 and 9 for audio script.)

Track 02

Gary:	Hi, Paul. It's great to see you.
Paul:	Hiya, you too. How are things?
Gary:	Good, thanks. How are you doing?
Paul:	I'm very well, thanks. How was your journey?
Gary:	OK, thanks. The train was on time.

Track 03

(See page 10 for audio script.)

Tracks 04 and 05

(See page 11 for audio script.)

Track 06

1   Hi Steve, it's great to see you.
    [beep]
2   Ms Smith? I'm James Robertson. Lovely to meet you.
    [beep]
3   Hey Frank. How are things?
    [beep]
4   Let me introduce you to Jilly. Jilly, this is Max.
    [beep]

Unit 2   Describing people

Track 07

(See pages 12 and 13 for audio script.)

Track 08

[schwa sound]

Track 09

(See page 14 for audio script.)

Track 10

(See page 15 for audio script.)

Track 11

1 See that man over there? Do you know who he is?
   [beep]
2 You know Elaine's friend, Ana? What's she like?
   [beep]
3 Who are those people by the window? Do you know them?
   [beep]
4 See that group of people by the door. They're friends of Ben's. I think they're a funny bunch. Don't you?
   [beep]

Unit 3   Talking about things

Track 12

(See pages 16 and 17 for audio script.)

Track 13

1
A: Have you finished the essay? I lost my notes from the lecture and there are so many things I can't remember.
B: Don't worry. I've got hundreds of books and notes.
A: Really? Can I borrow them, please?
B: Of course. They're in that sort of silvery folder on my desk.

2
A: Is it OK if I leave my stuff here?
B: Yes, of course You've got tonnes of bags. What have you bought?
A: Just some things for Helen's party. Did you find a nice birthday present for her?
B: Yeah, I got this. It's a kind of notebook and diary for college.

Track 14

(See page 18 for audio script.)

Track 15

(See page 19 for audio script.)

Tracks 16 and 17

(See page 19 for audio script.)

Track 18

1 What have you got in these boxes?
   [beep]
2 How old is this necklace?
   [beep]

3 How many pairs of shoes have you got?
   [beep]
4 What's your favourite item of clothing?
   [beep]
5 Have you got lots of English textbooks?
   [beep]

Unit 4   Talking about places

Track 19

(See pages 20 and 21 for audio script.)

Track 20

1 The big park in the centre of town?
2 You know Trafalgar Square?
3 You know where the canteen is?
4 See the park at the end of the street?

Track 21

(See page 22 for audio script.)

Tracks 22 and 23

(See page 23 for audio script.)

Track 24

1 Excuse me, I'm looking for the reception desk.
   [beep]
2 Hi, do you know where the train station is?
   [beep]
3 Excuse me, is there a good cafe round here?
   [beep]

Unit 5   Making arrangements

Track 25

(See pages 24 and 25 for audio script.)

Track 26

(See page 27 for audio script.)

Track 27

[beep]
Hi, yes. What time shall I pick you up?
[beep]

OK, great. I'll pick you up then.

[beep]

Track 28

Hello. Are you still free for coffee today?

[beep]

OK. No problem.

[beep]

Bye.

Track 29

Hello. I'm phoning to finalise dates for the department meeting. Would you be able to attend on Tuesday or Wednesday?

[beep]

Great. Shall we say about 10 a.m.?

[beep]

Thank you. I'll email you directions and details now. Look forward to seeing you then.

[beep]

Bye.

Unit 6   Making requests

Track 30

(See pages 28 and 29 for audio script.)

Track 31

(See page 30 for audio script.)

Tracks 32 and 33

(See page 30 for audio script.)

Track 34

1   That's fine. Remember to come home by 10, please.
2   Sorry, I'm waiting for a friend.
3   Of course. Here you are.
4   Sorry, I'll move my bag for you.
5   No problem. Write your personal details here, your registration details here, and your student module numbers here.
6   Well, I'll need it for Monday afternoon at the latest. Get it to me before lunchtime, please.

Unit 7   Ordering and buying

Track 35

(See pages 32 and 33 for audio script.)

Track 36

A: Do you have any tickets for Popfest?

B: Yes, how many would you like?

A: Four, please. How much are they?

B: They're £50 for the VIP seats.

A: That's very expensive.

B: Well, we do have standing tickets. They're only £20 each.

A: That sounds good. I'll take those, please.

B: OK. That's £80, please. Thank you. And here are your tickets.

A: Thank you.

Track 37

1   The tickets are twenty quid each.
2   So, one coffee and one pastry. That's four fifty altogether.
3   I'm not sure how much dinner cost. I think it was fifty pounds.
4   The evening course is a hundred pounds per month.

Track 38

1   six pounds and fifteen pee; six pounds fifteen; six fifteen
2   eighty quid; eighty pounds
3   one hundred pounds; a hundred pounds; a hundred quid
4   seven pounds and fifty pence; seven pounds fifty; seven fifty

Track 39

1   seven forty-five; quarter to eight
2   half past six; half six; six thirty
3   nine; nine a.m. or nine p.m.; nine o'clock

Track 40

1   Let me see. OK, that sounds good.
2   Let me think. I'll take those, please.

Track 41

(See page 35 for audio script.)

Track 42

1
[beep]
Hello, let me see... Yes, we have one place left.
[beep]
It's £615 for one month.
[beep]
OK. Would you like to pay for your place now or leave a deposit?
[beep]
2
[beep]

Yes, we have a few tickets.

[beep]

We have tickets for £75 and we have tickets for £50 at the back.

[beep]

Certainly. That's £150 please.

3

Hi, what can I get you?

[beep]

OK, anything else? Something to eat?

[beep]

Certainly. To have in or take away?

[beep]

Unit 8   Speaking on the phone

Track 43

(See pages 36 and 37 for audio script.)

Track 44

1 Hi, this is Sylvia. Sorry I can't take your call.
2 I'll get back to you.
3 Call me when you get this message.
4 Can I speak to Mrs Plant?
5 Listen, I'm not interested.
6 Can you hear me now?
7 Sorry, I didn't catch that.
8 The line is terrible.

Track 45

(See page 38 for audio script.)

Track 46

(See page 38 for audio script.)

Track 47

(See page 38 for audio script.)

Track 48

Mr Dawson: Er, thank you, but I, um, don't want to change contract.

[beep]

Mr Dawson: Mmmm, no, I'm sorry, I'm really not interested.

[beep]

Mr Dawson: Listen, I'm not interested. Now thank you for calling, but my answer is no. Goodbye.

[beep]

Track 49

1

Hi, sorry I can't take your call. Leave your name and a short message, and I'll call you back. Thanks.

[beep]

2

Hi, how are you? Hello? Sorry, the reception's bad on my mobile. What are you doing tonight?

[beep]

What are you doing tonight? Do you want to go to the cinema?

[beep]

Sorry, do you want to come to the cinema tonight?

[beep]

OK, see you then.

3

Hello, I'm phoning from Top Mobile. My name's Simon. I'm phoning to offer you a very exciting new contract.

[beep]

This is a great opportunity to save money and to get a new mobile.

[beep]

You need to make one small payment. You don't want to miss this opportunity.

[beep]

Unit 9   Showing interest in a conversation

Track 50

(See pages 40 and 41 for audio script.)

Track 51

(See page 42 for audio script.)

Tracks 52 and 53

(See page 43 for audio script.)

Track 54

(See page 43 for audio script.)

Track 55

1

Can I sit here? Oh, what a busy morning! I went to work at 6 a.m. I'm so tired.

[beep]

My boss is away at the moment. We're working extra hours. It's terrible.

[beep]

I don't like my job. I'm looking for another job.

[beep]

2

Hey, guess what? I've got two job offers for part-time work!

[beep]

The first job is a teaching assistant at the college. They give me free language classes, too.

[beep]

The other job is working as a waitress at the new cafe in town.

[beep]

3

Hi, I'm glad I caught you. Have you got a minute?

[beep]

Oh. Do you have to go now? I wanted to have a chat.

[beep]

Unit 10   Developing a conversation

Track 56

(See pages 44 and 45 for audio script.)

Track 57

(See page 46 for audio script.)

Track 58

(See page 47 for audio script.)

Track 59

(See page 47 for audio script.)

Track 60

1

I didn't like that trip.

[beep]

And the weather was bad, wasn't it?

[beep]

What I did like was the people. They were nice.

[beep]

2

Wow! What a great course. I loved it!

[beep]

I'm looking forward to working on this project.

[beep]

The new boss is really good, isn't she?

[beep]

Unit 11   Checking for understanding

Track 61

(See pages 48 and 49 for audio script.)

Track 62

(See page 50 for audio script.)

Track 63

(See page 51 for audio script.)

Track 64

(See page 51 for audio script.)

Track 65

1

Now, this is an important task. It's very easy. Click the green button to start and then enter your password.
[beep]
Yeah. Then we can check the data here is correct.
[beep]
2
I have to complete one essay and one project for next week. Which one do I start first? What do you think?
[beep]
Sorry, I don't get it.
[beep]
Oh, I see. Thanks!

Unit 12   Listening to problems

Track 66

(See pages 52 and 53 for audio script.)

Track 67

(See page 54 for audio script.)

Track 68

(See page 55 for audio script.)

Track 69

1

I'm not enjoying my course. I don't like my teacher, either. He gives me really low marks for all my work.
[beep]
Mmmm, I don't know what to do. I can't talk to mum and dad about it. They're paying for the course.
[beep]

2

Are you sure you've got everything? It's a very big city. I'm worried about you.

[beep]

Call me when you get there. Try to meet some friends, but go to bed early, too.

[beep]

Unit 13   Making a complaint

Track 70

(See page pages 56 and 57 for audio script.)

Track 71

(See page 58 for audio script.)

Tracks 72 and 73

(See page 59 for audio script.)

Track 74

1

[beep]

Oh dear. I'm very sorry about that. Can I offer you a full refund or an exchange?

[beep]

No problem. Do you have the receipt?

[beep]

That's great. Thank you. Let me get you a mobile from the storeroom for your exchange.

2

Here you are. The fish for you, sir. And the vegetarian for you, madam.

[beep]

Oh, did you? I'll change that for you.

[beep]

I'm very sorry. I'm afraid, we're very busy today. But I'll tell the chef and he'll prepare fresh meals for you.

[beep]

I really am very sorry.

[beep]

Unit 14   Making an apology

Track 75

(See pages 60 and 61 for audio script.)

Track 76

(See page 62 for audio script.)

Tracks 77 and 78

(See page 63 for audio script.)

Track 79

1

What happened yesterday? You shouted at me and I don't know why. You were horrible.

[beep]

You were really rude to me.

[beep]

Well, I don't want to fall out over it.

2

Hey, how's things? Sorry, I'm late. The traffic's bad today.

[beep]

I'm really sorry. Can I make it up to you?

[beep]

3

[beep]

Yes, OK. I've got five minutes.

[beep]

No problem. Don't worry about it. We all make mistakes.

Unit 15   Showing sympathy

Track 80

(See pages 64 and 65 for audio script.)

Track 81

(See page 66 for audio script.)

Track 82

(See page 67 for audio script.)

Track 83

1

Thanks for coming to visit me.

[beep]

Thanks. It's very painful. The accident was terrible. I was pretty scared.

[beep]

2

I failed a test today. I can't believe it.

[beep]

I feel so stupid. I just couldn't remember anything, so I made lots of little mistakes. I was really nervous.

[beep]

3

[beep]

Oh no. I don't understand – it's perfect for me. That's really disappointing.

[beep]

Unit 16   Saying 'thank you'

Track 84

(See pages 68 and 69 for audio script.)

Tracks 85, 86 and 87

(See page 70 for audio script.)

Track 88

(See page 71 for audio script.)

Track 89

1

Ok, here are the notes for the presentation. I think it's finished now.

[beep]

No problem.

2

Congratulations on your graduation. We're very proud. Did you like your present?

[beep]

Oh, you're welcome.

3

Are you free on Saturday? I'm having a party.

[beep]

Oh, that's a shame.

Track 90

1

Thanks. I'm really thirsty.

[beep]

2

Thanks for the lift home. I appreciate it.

[beep]

3

That was delicious! Thank you so much for lunch.

[beep]

Unit 17   Agreeing and disagreeing

Track 91

(See page 72 for audio script.)

Track 92

(See page 74 for audio script.)

Track 93

(See page 75 for audio script.)

Track 94

1

So what did you think of the album?

[beep]

Mmm. I love this track. Don't you? It's my favourite.

[beep]

Why? It's brilliant. It's number one this week in the charts!

[beep]

2

Can you explain the comment you wrote on my essay?

[beep]

Ah, I see. I don't know when to use formal language. It's very difficult.

[beep]

Oh, yes, OK. I'm going to look at my notes from the lesson.

Unit 18   Stronger opinions

Track 95

(See pages 76 and 77 for audio script.)

Track 96

(See page 78 for audio script.)

Track 97

(See page 78 for audio script.)

Track 98

(See page 79 for audio script.)

Track 99

(See page 79 for audio script.)

1

I love my car. It's very important to me. It's the best way to travel.

[beep]

I travelled by bus last year and they were always late or busy. I can use my car any time. So I use it every day, for work or for going out.

[beep]

Yes, I know. But it's the best way to travel for me. I work long hours and I travel with my work, so I can't use public transport. It's really my only option.

[beep]

2

Are you studying again? I think you study too hard.

[beep]

What I'm trying to say is you study a lot. You didn't come to the party last week. We're all going out tonight but you're studying again instead. Have some fun!

[beep]

I know. But you can have some time off. It's good to relax, too.

[beep]

Unit 19   Giving feedback

Track 101

(See pages 80 and 81 for audio script.)

Track 102

(See page 82 for audio script.)

Track 103

(See page 82 for audio script.)

Track 104

(See page 83 for audio script.)

Track 105

1

I bought this coat yesterday. It was really expensive. What do you think?

[beep]

Oh, I really like it. What's wrong with it?

[beep]

2

[beep]

Sure. What's wrong?

[beep]

Why? I'm just texting and chatting. Everybody uses mobiles.

[beep]

Unit 20   Saying 'Well done!'

Track 106

(See pages 84 and 85 for audio script.)

Track 107

(See page 86 for audio script.)

Track 108

(See page 86 for audio script.)

Track 109

(See page 86 for audio script.)

Tracks 110 and 111

(See page 87 for audio script.)

Track 112

1

Guess what? I passed my school exams!

[beep]

Thank you. I'm so excited. I studied really hard for these exams. It's a big relief.

[beep]

2

[beep]

Wow! Well done! You deserve it. I'm proud of you.

[beep]

3

Have you heard? I'm getting married!

[beep]

Thanks. We're choosing the date and trying to organise things.

[beep]

I'm so happy. I can't wait!